THE MACMILLAN BOOK OF EARLIEST CHRISTIAN PRAYERS

THE

MACMILLAN BOOK OF

EARLIEST CHRISTIAN PRAYERS

EDITED BY

F. Forrester Church

AND

Terrence J. Mulry

Macmillan Publishing Company
NEW YORK
Collier Macmillan Publishers
LONDON

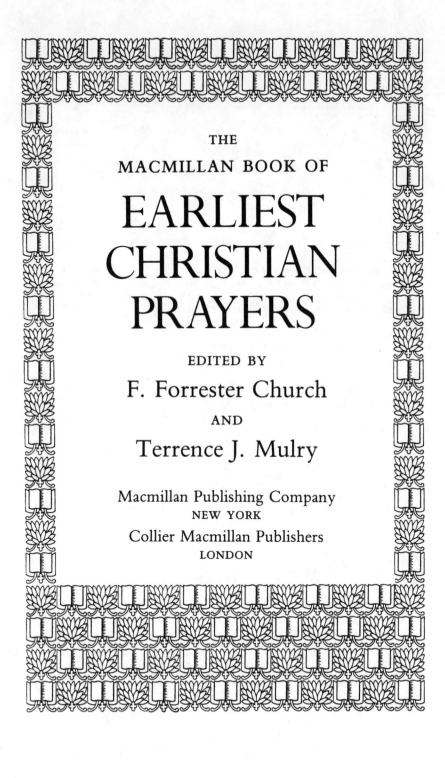

Macmillan Publishing Company
866 Third Avenue, New York, NY 10022
Collier Macmillan Canada, Inc.

Library of Congress Cataloging-in-Publication Data
The Macmillan book of earliest Christian prayers.
1. Prayers, Early Christian. I. Church, F. Forrest.
II. Mulry, Terrence.
BV236.M33 1988 242′.8011 87-28233

ISBN 0-02-525570-3

10 9 8 7 6 5 4 3 2 1

Printed in the United States of America

CONTENTS

PREFACE

If you wish to enter the chancel of a person's soul, the most direct passageway is through his or her prayers. This is certainly true of early Christian prayers. Artful yet without artifice, each is an intimate conversation with God, deep calling unto deep, transforming language itself into a sacrament. When we partake of it, even at the distance of almost two millennia, this communion between believer and God has transformational power. On the aspirational altar of these early Christians, we discover holy and mysterious elements to nurture our souls as well.

When we stepped back to edit this volume—I from my pastoral duties at All Souls Unitarian Church in New York City, and Terrence J. Mulry from his studies at Harvard Divinity School—instead of pouring our spirits into an old wineskin, we were refreshed in an encounter that not only brought the past alive, but the present also. It may only be an innocent illusion, but we discovered that many of these prayers, profound from the moment of their first utterance, actually seem to improve with age. Perhaps this is because every time a prayer touches a new life, its power is extended.

As with all great devotional literature, these prayers are timeless. Conditions may change from one generation to another, but not the human condition itself, the mystery of being alive and having to die. Although Saint Paul, Saint Augustine, and the others did not have us in mind when they wrote them, in quiet moments centuries later their prayers speak directly to our hearts and address our deepest needs.

This collection is the first of three, with anthologies of the earliest Christian hymns and meditations soon to follow. Tapping into the rich vein of early Christian literature, our hope is that together these books will provide a valuable source for daily devotional refreshment.

We have not designed them for scholars, except as a resource for their own devotions. After all, libraries filled with specialized books for reference and study are available to scholars of early Christian literature. In assembling these materials we have depended greatly upon such resources. But rather than duplicating or pretending to duplicate them, each of these volumes is fashioned to provide a companionable collection of ancient prayers, hymns, or meditations for nonspecialists, among whom we number ourselves.

Since our intended readers are those who seek to extend their acquaintance with Christian literature while cultivating their own spiritual gardens, annotation is kept to a minimum. By the same token, when forced to choose, we favor poetic over literal translations.

We have no pretensions concerning our selections. While trying to be as inclusive as possible, marginal and dated material—those prayers that might advance scholarly understanding more than encourage spiritual growth—have been excluded.

Some of the prayers we do include will speak more directly to you than others. Early Christianity was as richly various in doctrine and expression as Christianity is today. Thus we have assembled a quilt of many traditions, basing our selections on the principle that a theologically diverse anthology of the devotional classics of early Christianity will prove more representative, illuminating, and challenging than one that reflects only the mainstream of Christian tradition.

This means, among other things, that we have chosen to include material not usually considered for devotional anthologies, such as the prayers drawn from the New Testament Apocrypha and Gnostic prayers from the Nag Hammadi Library, a major new resource for our appreciation of the varieties of early Christian experience. In this wealth of diversity we hope that you will chance upon priceless gems in surprising places.

For the first two centuries, we have included almost all of the major surviving prayers. For the prayers of the third, fourth, and fifth centuries, we had to be more selective, but always with an eye to ensuring that our choices would be representative. If some favorite early prayer appears to be missing, remember that many Christian prayers (beginning with the Magnifica of Mary in the Gospel of Luke and including several prayers in the Book of Revelation) are actually hymns or psalms, and so will appear in the second volume of this series. This volume does contain a wide selection of early liturgies, however, most of which feature brief hymns within their compass.

This volume is arranged in five major sections, each with three chapters.

Section I, "The First Christian Prayers," opens with selections from the New Testament and continues with a selection of second-century prayers from the Apostolic Fathers and papyri, as well as a sampling of prayers from the Nag Hammadi Library, some much earlier than others but all expressive of an early strain of Christian belief.

Section II, "The Church Comes of Age," is composed for the most part of third-century prayers from the teachers of the established church, from the New Testament Apocrypha (writings under the names of disciples and apostles representative of various other traditions of early Christian teaching), and from the earliest Christian liturgies, reflecting worship practices in the first three centuries.

Section III, "Post-Nicene Prayers," contains choices from the fourth- and fifth-century Fathers (and Mothers) of the Church, most dating to the period following the Council of Nicea in 325, which coincidentally corresponds to the establishment of Christianity as the Roman state religion, upon the conversion of Constantine. These are arranged according to Greek, Syriac and Coptic, and Latin sources.

Section IV, "Liturgical Prayers East and West," is informed by the same principle of organization as Section III. Here, traditions of worship and theology that persist to this very day are clearly evident. Each tradition is distinctive, but many common elements unite the Eastern and Western liturgies with each other.

Section V, "The Prayers of Saint Augustine," marking the end of one era and the commencement of another, is devoted to prayers from the writings of Saint Augustine. Among the selections from his *Confessions,* sermons, commentaries, tractates, and *Soliloquies,* you will rediscover several of the most cherished prayers in the entire history of Christian literature.

At the end of the book you will find two indexes, one devotional and topical, the other a name and source index, to help make this anthology more accessible and useful as an aid for personal devotions.

We are indebted to many people for their encouragement and support in putting this volume together. Our thanks go, first, to Charles Scribner III, vice president of Macmillan Publishing Company, who conceived this idea and kindly invited us to consider the possibility of editing this series, and also to Stephen Wilburn, director of Religious Books, who enthusiastically embraced the concept and was a prime mover in shepherding it from dream to reality.

Many others provided advice and assistance. We especially thank Anne Carr, University of Chicago Divinity School; Brian Daly, Weston School of Theology; Robert M. Grant, University of Chicago Divinity School; Holland Hendrix, Barnard College; Seth Kasten, Union Theological Seminary; Helmut Koester, Harvard University Divinity School; Dennis R. MacDonald, Iliff School of Theology; Stanley B. Marrow, Weston School of Theology; Wayne A. Meeks, Yale Divinity School; Kathleen McVey, Princeton Theological Seminary; Margaret Miles, Harvard Divinity School; Roland E. Murphy, Duke Divinity School; Jaroslav Pelikan, Yale University; Louke van Wensveen, Princeton Theological Seminary; Geoffrey Wainright, Duke Divinity School; and Lawrence Wills, Harvard Divinity School.

Most of the prayers included here were translated in the nineteenth and early twentieth century and are therefore in the public domain. We do express our appreciation for permission to reproduce more recently translated prayers from the following sources: *The Fathers of the Church,* Thomas P. Halton, et. al., editors (Washington, D.C.: The Catholic University of America Press), Vols. 22, 23, 44, 51, 64, 71, 74, 75; *Early Christian Prayers,* edited by A. Hammon, with English translation by Walter Mitchell (Chicago: Henry Regnery Company, 1961); *New Testament Apocrypha II,* Edgar Hennecke, edited by Wilhelm Schneemelcher, with

English translation edited by R. Mcl. Wilson (Philadelphia: The Westminster Press, 1965); *Ancient Christian Writers,* Vol. 6, James A. Kleist, translator (Westminster, Md.: The Newman Press, 1948); *The Nag Hammadi Library in English,* James M. Robinson, et. al., editors and translators (New York: Harper & Row, 1977).

For those wishing to extend their acquaintance with the devotional literature of the first five centuries of Christianity, among the many fine books available we especially recommend: Hammon's *Early Christian Prayers,* Lucien Deiss's *Springtime of the Liturgy* (The Liturgical Press, 1979), Lisa Sergio's *Prayers of Women* (Harper & Row, 1965), and Barry Ulanov's *Prayers of St. Augustine* (Seabury Press, 1983).

With deep appreciation we dedicate this volume to the congregations of The Unitarian Church of All Souls in New York City and The First Church of Belmont, Massachusetts, with whom we pray.

F. Forrester Church

I. The First Christian Prayers

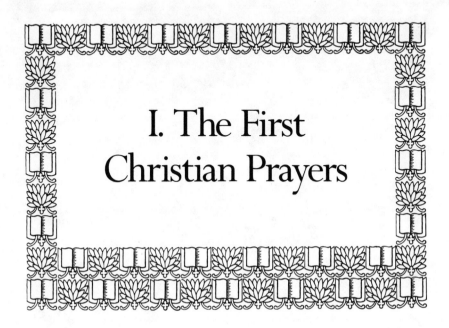

ANY questions concerning the centrality of prayer to Jesus, his disciples, and the first Christian communities are answered eloquently within the New Testament itself. From the wilderness to Gethsemane, Jesus devotes many of his most precious hours to prayer. In the Sermon on the Mount he teaches his followers how to pray (Matt. 6:5–15), urging them not to make a display of their piety, either through public demonstration or the heaping up of empty phrases, but rather to pray simply and in private "to your Father who is in secret, and your Father who sees in secret will reward you." Jesus' farewell discourse is cast in the form of a prayer (John 17), and as he dies, on his lips are prayers of lamentation (Matt. 27:46), intercession for those who have wronged him (Luke 23:32), and consecration (Luke 23:46). Following in this same spirit, each of Paul's letters begins with a prayer of thanksgiving, and the book of Acts is filled with prayerful encounters. In fact, every book in the New Testament either contains a prayer or alludes to prayer within the early Christian community.

Other writings dating to the time when the New Testament books were written and shortly thereafter continue this same tradition. In Chapter Two, we include late first- and second-century prayers from the Apostolic Fathers. The prayer that closes the first epistle of Clement of Rome is the longest and among the finest of early Christian prayers, and that of Polycarp, recorded in the earliest extant Acts of the Christian Martyrs, evinces the resolve and expectancy of early Christian martyrs. The papyri prayers cannot be dated exactly, but each reflects ancient Christian practice.

The prayers from Nag Hammadi, contained in Chapter Three, are also difficult to date, but in spirit they either reflect various schools of early Gnostic Christianity stemming from the first century, or non-Christian Gnostic Schools that directly influenced the development of Gnostic Christianity. Here, knowledge (*gnosis*) holds priority over faith or belief. This split within early Christian theology is recorded in Paul's letters, but many scholars also find direct evidence of Gnostic, or proto-Gnostic, teaching in the New Testament, especially in the Gospel of John. In Gnostic theology, Christ's mission is to awaken those who possess the light of divinity to their own godhood, that they may be released from the prison of matter and return to the divine realm from whence they came. But theology aside, several of these prayers are accessible to the modern reader and profoundly moving. Note particularly their ecstatic character. Some even contain the earliest examples of *glossolalia,* or "speaking in tongues."

ONE

New Testament Prayers

OUR Father which art in heaven,
Hallowed be thy name.
Thy kingdom come,
Thy will be done,
In earth as it is in heaven.
Give us this day our daily bread.
And forgive us our debts,
As we forgive our debtors.
And lead us not into temptation,
But deliver us from evil.

MATTHEW 6:9–13

FATHER, I thank thee that thou hast heard me. And I knew that thou hearest me always: but because of the people which stand by, I said it that they may believe that thou hast sent me.

JOHN 11:41–42

I thank thee, O Father, Lord of Heaven and earth, that thou hast hid these things from the wise and prudent, and hast revealed them unto babes: even so, Father: for so it seemed good in thy sight.

LUKE 10:21

FATHER, the hour is come; glorify thy Son, that thy Son also may glorify thee:

As thou hast given him power over all flesh, that he should give eternal life to as many as thou hast given him.

And this is life eternal, that they might know thee the only true God, and Jesus Christ, whom thou hast sent.

I have glorified thee on the earth: I have finished the work which thou gavest me to do.

And now, O Father, glorify thou me with thine own self with the glory which I had with thee before the world was.

I have manifested thy name unto the men which thou gavest me out of the world: thine they were, and thou gavest them me; and they have kept thy word.

Now they have known that all things whatsoever thou hast given me are of thee.

For I have given unto them the words which thou gavest me; and they have received them, and have known surely that I came out from thee, and they have believed that thou didst send me.

I pray for them: I pray not for the world, but for them which thou hast given me; for they are thine.

And all mine are thine, and thine are mine; and I am glorified in them.

And now I am no more in the world, but these are in the world, and I come to thee. Holy Father, keep through thine own name those whom thou hast given me, that they may be one, as we are.

While I was with them in the world, I kept them in thy name: those that thou gavest me I have kept, and none of them is lost, but the son of perdition; that the Scripture might be fulfilled.

And now come I to thee; and these things I speak in the world, that they might have my joy fulfilled in themselves.

I have given them thy word; and the world hath hated them, because they are not of the world, even as I am not of the world.

I pray not that thou shouldest take them out of the world, but that thou shouldest keep them from the evil.

They are not of the world, even as I am not of the world.

Sanctify them through thy truth: thy word is truth.

As thou hast sent me into the world, even so have I also sent them into the world.

And for their sakes I sanctify myself, that they also might be sanctified through the truth.

Neither pray I for these alone, but for them also which shall believe on me through their word;

That they all may be one; as thou, Father, art in me, and I in thee, that they also may be one in us: that the world may believe that thou has sent me.

And the glory which thou gavest me I have given them; that they may be one, even as we are one:

I in them, and thou in me, that they may be made perfect in one; and that the world may know that thou hast sent me, and hast loved them, as thou hast loved me.

Father, I will that they also, whom thou hast given me, be with me where I am; that they may behold my glory, which thou hast given me: for thou lovedst me before the foundation of the world.

O righteous Father, the world hath not known thee:

but I have known thee, and these have known that thou hast sent me.

And I have declared unto them thy name, and will declare it: that the love wherewith thou hast loved me may be in them, and I in them.

JOHN 17:1–26

O my Father, if it be possible, let this cup pass from me: nevertheless not as I will, but as thou wilt. . . .

O my Father, if this cup may not pass away from me, except I drink it, thy will be done. . . .

MATTHEW 26:39, 42

FATHER, forgive them; for they know not what they do. . . .

Father, into thy hands I commend my spirit.

LUKE 23:34, 46

GOD be merciful to me a sinner.

LUKE 18:13

LORD, thou art God, which hast made Heaven, and earth, and the sea, and all that in them is; who by the mouth of thy servant David hast said, Why did the heathen rage, and the people imagine vain things?

The kings of the earth stood up, and the rulers were gathered together against the Lord, and against his Christ. For of a truth against thy holy child Jesus, whom thou hast anointed, both Herod, and Pontius Pilate, with the Gentiles, and the people of Israel, were gathered together, for to do whatsoever thy hand and thy counsel determined before to be done.

And now, Lord, behold their threatenings: and grant unto thy servants, that with all boldness they may speak thy word, by stretching forth thine hand to heal; and that signs and wonders may be done by the name of thy holy child Jesus.

ACTS 4:24–30

LORD Jesus, receive my spirit. . . .
Lord, lay not this sin to their charge. . . .

ACTS 7:59, 60

O the depths of the riches both of the wisdom and knowledge of God! How unsearchable are his judgments, and his ways past finding out! For who hath known the mind of the Lord? Or who hath been his counselor? Or who hath first given to him, and it shall be recompensed unto him again? For of him, and through him, and to him, are all things: to whom be glory forever. Amen.

ROMANS 11:33–36

NOW the God of patience and consolation grant you to be likeminded one toward another according to Christ Jesus, that ye may with one mind and one mouth glorify God, even the Father of our Lord Jesus Christ. . . .

Now the God of hope fill you with all joy and peace in believing, that ye may abound in hope, through the power of the Holy Ghost. . . .

Now the God of peace be with you all. Amen.

ROMANS 15:5–6, 13, 33

BLESSED be God, even the Father of our Lord Jesus Christ, the Father of mercies, and the God of all comfort; who comforteth us in all our tribulations, that we may be able to comfort them which are in any trouble, by the comfort wherewith we ourselves are comforted of God. For as the sufferings of Christ abound in us, so our consolation also aboundeth by Christ.

2 CORINTHIANS 1:3–5

THE grace of the Lord Jesus Christ, and the love of God and the communion of the Holy Ghost be with you all. Amen.

2 CORINTHIANS 13:14

GRACE be to you and peace, from God the Father and from our Lord Jesus Christ, who gave himself for our sins, that he might deliver us from this present evil world, according to the will of God and our Father; to whom be glory for ever and ever. Amen.

GALATIANS 1:3–4

I thank my God upon every remembrance of you, always in every prayer of mine for you all making request with joy, for your fellowship in the Gospel from the first day until now, being confident of this very thing, that he which hath begun a good work in you will perform it until the day of Jesus Christ: even as it is meet for me to think this of you all, because I have you in my heart, inasmuch as both in my bonds, and in the defense and confirmation of the Gospel, ye all are partakers of my grace. For God is my record, how greatly I long after you all in the bowels of Jesus Christ. And this I pray, that your love may abound yet more and more in knowledge and in all judgment, that ye may approve things that are excellent, that ye may be sincere and without offense till the day of Christ, being filled with the fruits of righteousness, which are by Jesus Christ, unto the glory and praise of God.

PHILIPPIANS 1:3–11

NOW God himself and our Father, and our Lord Jesus Christ, direct our way unto you. And the Lord make you to increase and abound in love one toward another, and toward all men, even as we do toward you: to the end he may stablish your hearts unblamable in holiness before God, even our Father, at the coming of our Lord Jesus Christ with all his saints.

1 THESSALONIANS 3:11–13

MAY the very God of peace sanctify you wholly; and I pray God your whole spirit and soul and body be preserved blameless unto the coming of our Lord Jesus Christ.

1 THESSALONIANS 5:23

NOW our Lord Jesus Christ himself, and God, even our Father, which hath loved us, and hath given us everlasting consolation and good hope through grace, comfort your hearts, and stablish you in every good word and work.

2 THESSALONIANS 2:16–17

FOR this cause we also, since the day we heard it, do not cease to pray for you, and to desire that ye might be filled with the knowledge of his will in all wisdom and spiritual understanding, that ye might walk worthy of the Lord unto all pleasing, being fruitful in every good work, and increasing in the knowledge of God, strengthened with all might, according to his glorious power, unto all patience and longsuffering with joyfulness, giving thanks unto the Father, which hath made us meet to be partakers of the inheritance of the Saints in light, who hath delivered us from the power of darkness, and hath translated us into the kingdom of his dear Son, in whom we have redemption through his blood, even the forgiveness of sins.

COLOSSIANS 1:9–14

BLESSED be the God and Father of our Lord Jesus Christ, who hath blessed us with all spiritual blessings in heavenly places in Christ, according as he hath chosen us in him before the foundation of the world, that we should be holy and without blame before him in love, having predestinated us unto the adoption of children by Jesus Christ to himself, according to the good pleasure of his will, to the praise of the glory of his grace, wherein he hath made us accepted in the beloved, in whom we have redemption through his blood, the forgiveness of sins, according to the riches of his grace, wherein he hath abounded toward us in all wisdom and prudence, having made known unto us the mystery of his will, according to his good pleasure which he hath purposed in himself, that in the dispensation of the fullness of times he might gather together in one all things in Christ, both which are in Heaven, and which are on earth, even in him, in whom also we have obtained an inheritance, being predestinated according to the purpose of him who worketh all things after the counsel of his own will, that we should be to the praise of his glory, who first trusted in Christ.

In whom ye also trusted, after that ye heard the word of truth, the Gospel of your salvation, in whom also, after that ye believed, ye were sealed with that Holy Spirit of promise, which is the earnest of our inheritance until the redemption of the purchased possession, unto the praise of his glory.

Wherefore I also, after I heard of your faith in the Lord Jesus, and love unto all the saints, cease not to give thanks for you, making mention of you in my prayers, that the God of our Lord Jesus Christ, the Father of glory, may give unto you the spirit of wisdom and revelation in the knowledge of him, the eyes of your understanding being enlightened, that ye may know what is the hope of his calling, and what the riches of the glory of his inheritance in the saints, and what is the exceeding greatness of his power to usward who believe, according to the working of his mighty power, which he wrought in Christ, when he raised him from the dead, and set him at his own right hand in the heavenly places, far above all principality, and power, and might, and dominion, and every name that is named, not only in this world, but also in that which is to come, and hath put all things under his feet, and gave him to be the head over all things to the church, which is his body, the fullness of him that filleth all in all.

EPHESIANS 1:3–23

FOR this cause I bow my knees unto the Father of our Lord Jesus Christ, of whom the whole family in Heaven and earth is named, that he would grant you, according to the riches of his glory, to be strengthened with might by his Spirit in the inner man, that Christ may dwell in your hearts by faith, that ye, being rooted and grounded in love, may be able to comprehend with all saints what is the breadth, and length, and depth, and height, and to know the love of Christ, which passeth knowledge, that ye might be filled with all the fullness of God.

Now unto him that is able to do exceeding abundantly above all that we ask or think, according to the power that worketh in us, unto him be glory in the church by Christ Jesus throughout all ages, world without end. Amen.

EPHESIANS 3:14–21

NOW the God of peace, that brought again from the dead our Lord Jesus, that great shepherd of the sheep, through the blood of the everlasting convenant, make you perfect in every good work to do his will, working in you that which is well pleasing in his sight, through Jesus Christ, to whom be glory for ever and ever. Amen.

HEBREWS 13:20–21

THE blessed and only Potentate, the King of kings and Lord of lords, who only hath immortality, dwelling in the light which no man can approach unto, whom no man hath seen, nor can see. To whom be honor and power everlasting. Amen.

1 TIMOTHY 6:15–16

BLESSED be the God and Father of our Lord Jesus Christ, which according to his abundant mercy hath begotten us again unto a lively hope by the resurrection of Jesus Christ from the dead, to an inheritance incorruptible, and undefiled, and that fadeth not away, reserved in heaven for you, who are kept by the power of God through faith unto salvation ready to be revealed in the last time.

1 PETER 1:3–5

NOW unto him who is able to keep you from falling, and to present you faultless before the presence of his glory with exceeding joy to the only wise God our Saviour, be glory and majesty, dominion and power, both now and forever. Amen.

JUDE 24–25

T W O

Second-Century Prayers

WE shall ask with earnest prayer and supplication that the Creator of all may keep unbroken the fixed number of his elect in all the world through his beloved servant Jesus Christ, through whom he called us from darkness to light, from ignorance to knowledge of the glory of his name. Grant us, Lord, to hope on his name which is the basic principle of all creation, opening the eyes of our heart to know thee, who alone art highest in the highest, abiding holy among the holy ones. Thou humblest the insolence of the proud, destroying the imaginations of the Gentiles, lifting the humble aloft and humbling the lofty, making rich and making poor, killing and making alive, the only Benefactor of spirits and God of all flesh. Thou lookest into the abyss, Observer of men's works, Helper of those in danger, Saviour of those in despair, Creator and Overseer of every spirit. Thou increasest the nations on earth and didst choose out of them all those that love thee through Jesus Christ thy beloved Servant, through whom thou has trained, sanctified, and honored us. We beseech thee, Lord, to become our helper and protector. Save those of us in affliction, have mercy on the humble, raise the fallen, show thyself to those who are in need, heal the sick, turn back the wanderers of thy people, feed the hungry, ransom our prisoners, raise up the weak, comfort the feeblehearted. Let all the Gentiles know thee, that thou art God alone, and that Jesus Christ is thy Servant, and that "we are thy people and the sheep of thy pasture."

For thou didst make manifest the everlasting constitution of the world through the forces set in operation. Thou, Lord, didst create the world. Thou who art faithful in all generations, righteous in judgments, marvelous in strength and excellence, wise in creating and prudent in establishing all that was made, good in what is seen and kindly among them that trust in thee, merciful and pitiful—forgive our sins and unrighteousnesses, our trespasses and failings. Reckon not every sin of thy servants and handmaidens, but cleanse us with the cleansing of thy truth, and make our steps straight that we may walk in holiness and righteousness and simplicity of heart, and may do what things are good and well pleasing before thee and our governors. Yea, Lord, let thy face shine upon us for good in peace, that we may be sheltered by thy strong hand and delivered from all sin by thine uplifted arm, and deliver us from those that hate us unrighteously. Give concord and peace to us and to all the dwellers upon earth, as thou didst give to our fathers, when they called upon thee reverently in faith and truth, so that we may be saved, and grant that we may be obedient to thy almighty and excellent name, and to our governors and rulers on earth.

Thou, Lord, hast given them the authority of the Kingdom by thy excellent and unutterable might, that we, recognizing the glory and honor given them by thee, may be subject to them, in no respect opposing thy will. To them, Lord, grant health, peace, concord, stability, that they may administer the rule given them by thee without offense.

For thou, heavenly Lord, King of the ages, givest to the sons of men glory and honor, and authority over the things which are on earth. Do thou, Lord, direct their counsels according to what is good and well pleasing before thee, that piously administering in peace and gentleness the authority given them by thee they may obtain thy mercy. O thou who alone art able to do with us these good things and others more abundant, thee we praise through the high priest and protector of our souls, Jesus Christ, through whom be glory and majesty to thee both now and for all generations and for ever and ever. Amen.

CLEMENT OF ROME

ON you we call, Lord God,
all-wise, all-surveying, holy,
the only true Sovereign.
You created the universe,
you watch over all that exists.
Those that lie in darkness,
overshadowed by death,
you guide into the right road, the safe road.
Your will is that all men should be saved
and come to knowledge of the truth.

With one voice we offer you
praise and thanksgiving;
full-hearted, full-throated we sing you
the hymn you have a right to at this hour.
In your mercy you called to us
(holy the calling!),
taught us and trained us,
gave understanding, wisdom, truth to us,
life eternal.

You bought us back
with the pure and precious blood
of your only Son,
freed us from lies and error,
from bitter enslavement,
released us from the Devil's clutches
and gave us the glory of freedom.
We were dead and you renewed the life
of our souls and bodies in the Spirit.
We were soiled and you made us quite spotless again.

We pray you, merciful Father,
God from whom all encouragement comes,
give us strength to act as befits men with such a vocation,
such calling to worship, such newness of life.
We mean to observe the sacred commands
of the divine law;
we long to come closer to you, closer today,
long to have light from you, light to know you and serve
you.

We pray you, give us the strength
to do all this with a will.
Do not think of the sins we have committed
or of those we still commit.
Put out of your mind the failings we give way to
night and day.
Do not impute our offenses to us,
whether we did them on purpose
or whether we could not help them.
Remember, Lord,
that men are apt to make slips;
we are a spineless race, given to blundering:
think of our build, our limitations.
Our skins may be sound, but there are sores underneath.

O God, you are well disposed to us:
give us the strength of your support.
Give us encouragement, give the light that goes with it.
Make us live by the dogmas of the faith
preached by your holy apostles
and the high teaching of the Gospels
of our Saviour, Jesus Christ.

May we not be content only to hear and to speak of them
but behave and act as they bid us,
for then our conduct will deserve reward.

Teach us to look upwards, to seek out and probe the
heavenly,
not the earthly.
If that is our attitude and if you act in us,
what glory for your power,
all-holy, omnipotent, worthy of all praise;
glory through Jesus Christ, your beloved,
with the Holy Spirit,
now and throughout the ages.
Amen.

OUCHMOUNEN PAPYRUS

O God Almighty, who madest
Heaven and earth and sea and all that is therein,
help me, have mercy upon me, wash away my sins,
save me in this world and in the world to come,
through our Lord and Saviour Jesus Christ,
through whom is the glory and the power for
ever and ever. Amen.

OXYRHYNCHUS PAPYRUS

HELPER of men who turn to you,
Light of men in the dark,
Creator of all that grows from seed,
Promoter of all spiritual growth,
have mercy, Lord, on me
and make me a temple fit for yourself.
Do not scan my transgressions too closely,
for if you are quick to notice my offenses,
I shall not dare to appear before you.
In your great mercy,
in your boundless compassion,
wash away my sins, through Jesus Christ,
your only Child, the truly holy,
the chief of our souls' healers.
Through him may all glory be given you,
all power and honor and praise,
throughout the ending succession
of ages. Amen.

BERLIN PAPYRUS

THOU God and Father of thy beloved and blessed Son, our Lord Jesus Christ, through whom we have received knowledge of thee, O God of the angels and powers and of all creation and of all just men who live in thy presence, I thank thee that thou hast graciously vouchsafed this day and this hour to allot me a portion among the number of martyrs, among the people of Christ, unto the resurrection of everlasting life: among these may I be received in thy sight, this day, as a fruitful and acceptable sacrifice, wherefore, for all this, I praise thee, I bless thee, I glorify thee through the eternal High Priest, Jesus Christ, thy beloved Son; to whom, with thee and the Holy Ghost, be all glory, world without end. Amen.

SAINT POLYCARP

TRULY fearless, truly fortunate martyrs, called and chosen to glorify our Lord Jesus Christ! If any man magnifies the Lord, honors and adores him, these are the models for him. If he reads about them, he will find that though they are modern, they are not inferior to the ancient ones: they will edify the Church just as much. These new examples of virtue will prove that it is one and the same Holy Spirit who was active then and is active now, one and the same omnipotent God the Father and his Son, Jesus Christ, our Lord, whose glory and power are boundless and always will be, age after age. Amen.

TERTULLIAN

THREE

Prayers from Nag Hammadi

. . . YOUR light, give me your mercy!

My Redeemer, redeem me, for I am yours: from you have I come forth.

You are my mind: bring me forth!

You are my treasure house: open for me!

You are my fullness: take me to you!

You are my repose: give me the perfection that cannot be grasped!

I invoke you, the One who is and preexisted, by the name which is exalted above every name, through Jesus Christ the Lord of lords, the King of the ages: give me your gifts which you do not regret through the Son of man, the Spirit, the Paraclete of truth.

Give me authority when I ask you; give healing for my body when I ask you through the Evangelist, and redeem my eternal light-soul and my spirit.

And the Firstborn of the pleroma of grace—reveal him to my mind!

Grant what no angel eye has seen and no archon ear has heard and what has not entered into the human heart, which came to be angelic and came to be after the image of the psychic God when it was formed in the beginning, since I have faith and hope. And place upon me your beloved, elect, and blessed greatness, the Firstborn, the First-begotten, . . . and the wonderful mystery of your house; for yours is the power and the glory and the blessing and the greatness for ever and ever. Amen.

PRAYER OF THE APOSTLE PAUL

MY God and my Father,
who saved me from this dead hope,
who made me alive through a mystery of what he wills,
do not let these days of this world be prolonged for me,
but the day of your light . . . remains
in salvation.
Deliver me from this place of sojourn!
Do not let your grace be left behind in me,
but may your grace become pure!
Save me from an evil death!
Bring me from a tomb alive,
because your grace—love—is alive in me
to accomplish a work of fullness!
Save me from sinful flesh,
because I trusted in you with all my strength!
Because you are the life of the life,
save me from a humiliating enemy!
Do not give me into the hand of a judge
who is severe with sin!
Forgive me all my debts of the days of my life!
Because I am alive in you, your grace is alive in me.
I have renounced everyone,
but you I have confessed.
Save me from evil affliction!
But now is the time and the hour.

O Holy Spirit, send me
salvation . . . the light . . .
the light . . . in a power. . . .

THE SECOND APOCALYPSE OF JAMES

IĒ ieus ēō ou ēō ōua! Really truly, O Yesseus Mazareus Yessedekeus, O living water, O child of the child, O glorious name, really truly, aiōn o ōn (or: O existing aeon), iiii ēēēē eeee oo oo uuuu ōōōō aaaaa, really truly, ēi aaaa ōō ōō, O existing one who sees the aeons! Really truly, aee ēēē iiii uuuuuu ōōōōōōōō, who is eternally eternal, really truly, iēa aiō, in the heart, who exists, u aei eis aei, ei o ei ei os ei (or: Son forever, thou art what thou art, thou art who thou art)!

This great name of thine is upon me, O self-begotten perfect one, who art not outside me. I see thee, O thou who art invisible to everyone. For who will be able to comprehend thee in another tongue? Now that I have known thee, I have mixed myself with the immutable. I have armed myself with an armor of light; I have become light. For the Mother was at that place because of the splendid beauty of grace. Therefore I have stretched out my hands while they were folded. I was shaped in the circle of the riches of the light which is in my bosom, which gives shape to the many begotten ones in the light into which no complaint reaches. I shall declare thy glory truly, for I have comprehended thee, sou iēs ide aeiō aeie ois, O aeon, aeon, O God of silence! I honor thee completely. Thou art my place of rest, O son ēs ēs o e, the formless one who exists in the formless ones, who exists, raising up the man in whom thou wilt purify me into thy life, according to thine imperishable name. Therefore the incense of life is in me. I mixed it with water after the model of all archons, in order that I may live with thee in the peace of the saints, thou who existeth really truly forever.

THE GOSPEL OF THE EGYPTIANS

LET us pray, O my Father: I call upon thee, who rulest over the kingdom of power, whose word comes as [a] birth of light. And his words are immortal. They are eternal and unchanging. He is the one whose will begets life for the forms in every place. His nature gives form to substance. By him the souls of [the eighth and] the angels are moved . . . those that exist. His providence extends to everything . . . begets everything. He is the one who . . . the aeon among spirits. He created everything. He who is self-contained cares for everything. He is perfect, the invisible God to whom one speaks in silence—his image is moved when it is directed, and it governs—the one mighty in power, who is exalted above majesty, who is better than the honored ones, Zoxathazo a ōō ee ōōō ēēē ōōōō ēē ōōōōōō ooooo ōōōōōō uuuuuu ōōōōōōōōōōōō ōōō Zozazoth.

Lord, grant us a wisdom from thy power that reaches us, so that we may describe to ourselves the vision of the eighth and the ninth. We have already advanced to the seventh, since we are pious and walk in thy law. And thy will we fulfill always. For we have walked in thy way, and we have renounced . . . , so that thy vision may come. Lord, grant us the truth in the image. Allow us through the spirit to see the form of the image that has no deficiency, and receive the reflection of the pleroma from us through our praise.

And acknowledge the spirit that is in us. For from thee

the universe received soul. For from thee, the unbegotten one, the begotten one came into being. The birth of the self-begotten one is through thee, the birth of all begotten things that exist. Receive from us these spiritual sacrifices, which we send to thee with all our heart and our soul and all our strength. Save that which is in us, and grant us the immortal wisdom.

THE DISCOURSE ON THE EIGHTH AND NINTH

THOU art the root of the Light. Thy hidden form has appeared, O exalted, infinite One. May the whole power of the Spirit spread and may it be filled with its light, O infinite Light. [Then] he will not be able to join with the unbegotten Spirit, and the power of the astonishment will not be able to mix with Nature according to the will of the Majesty.

PARAPHRASE OF SHEM

O this great goodness of God! O Christ, King who has revealed to men the Great Divinity, King of every virtue and King of life, King of ages and Great One of the heavens, hear my words and forgive me!

TEACHING OF SILVANUS

THIS is the prayer that they spoke: "We give thanks to thee! Every soul and heart is lifted up to thee, O undisturbed Name, honored with the name 'God' and praised with the name 'Father,' for to everyone and everything comes the fatherly kindness and affection and love and any teaching there may be that is sweet and plain, giving us mind, speech, [and] knowledge: mind, so that we may understand thee, speech, so that we may expound thee, knowledge, so that we may know thee. We rejoice, having been illumined by thy knowledge. We rejoice because thou hast shown us thyself. We rejoice because while we were in the body, thou hast made us divine through thy knowledge.

"The delight of the man who attains to thee is one thing: that we know thee. We have known thee, O intellectual light. O Life of life, we have known thee. O womb of every creature, we have known thee. O womb pregnant with the nature of the Father, we have known thee. O eternal permanence of the begetting Father, thus have we worshiped thy goodness. There is one petition that we ask: we would be preserved in knowledge. And there is one protection that we desire: that we not stumble in this kind of life."

When they had said these things in prayer, they embraced each other and they went to eat their holy food, which has no blood in it.

PRAYER OF THANKSGIVING

I pray that I may never fall away from that knowledge of thee which matches with our being; grant thou this my prayer. And put power into me, that so, having obtained this boon, I may enlighten those of my race who are in ignorance, my brothers and thy sons.

CORPUS HERMETICUM

II. The Church Comes of Age

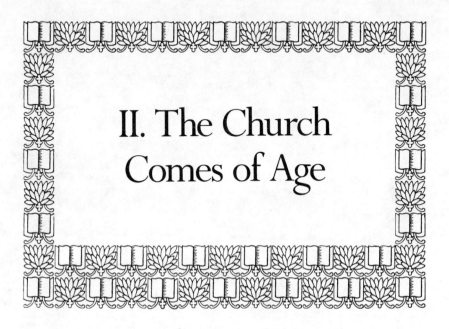

DURING the late second and the early third centuries, with Hippolytus, Ireneus, and Cyprian in the West and Clement of Alexandria and Origen in the East, most of the basic elements of what would emerge, with the Council of Nicea in 325, as orthodox Christian theology are developed fully for the first time, and certain distinctions between the Greek and Latin church become apparent. The former, directly influenced by pagan and Jewish Hellenistic philosophy and literature, was more speculative, metaphysical, and poetic; the latter, grounded deeply in the Old Testament and influenced by Latin rhetorical traditions, more pragmatic and prosaic. If the Latin fathers contribute more to the theological tradition later codified in the great councils of the church, the Alexandrian fathers, Clement and especially Origen, do more to advance the formal development of Christian devotions, directly influencing fourth- and fifth-century prayer in both the West and the East.

At the same time, more popular traditions are reflected in the books of the New Testament Apocrypha (Chapter Five), which stand in relation to the writings of the fathers in the same way that the legends of King Arthur do to the writings of the Venerable Bede, or as *Ben Hur* and *The Robe* do to the theological writings of Karl Barth and Hans Kung. That is, these works were read for pleasure as much as for edification. Accordingly, the prayers they contain are less orthodox in theological character but also have an exuberance and spontaneity lacking in the more formal prayers of the teachers of the Church. Each of these books is written under the pseudonym of a New Testament figure. This practice was common in the ancient world. Even in the New Testament itself, such writings as the Pastoral Epistles, which most scholars agree were written long after Paul's death, were penned under his name.

If we are to have a true picture of early Christian prayer, it must be framed in a liturgical context. Many of the prayers included in this volume were utilized in worship, and the development of liturgical traditions corresponds directly with that of early Christian prayer. In Chapter Six (opening with a background piece by Justin Martyr) we present several early liturgies and liturgical prayers, dating, with the Didache, back to the first century, all expressive of very early patterns of worship. Throughout, the central influence is the Jewish liturgy, where the pattern of alternating psalms, prayers, and lessons was first established. We include one prayer of Jewish origin (from the Didascalia) which was also used in Christian worship. Western liturgies are represented by the Apostolic Tradition of Hippolytus, Eastern by the Liturgy of Serapion and the Apostolic Constitutions; both trace their roots to the Didascalia, Didache, and Apostolic Tradition. The centerpiece of the Christian liturgy was the Eucharist, and eucharistic prayers, or anaphoras, number among the most beautiful and theologically telling of all early Christian prayers.

FOUR

Prayers of the Early Christian Fathers

O Educator, be gracious to thy children, O Educator, Father, Guide of Israel, Son and Father, both one, Lord. Give to us, who follow thy command, to fulfill the likeness of thy image, and to see, according to our strength, the God who is both a good God and a Judge who is not harsh. Do thou thyself bestow all things on us who dwell in thy peace, who have been placed in thy city, who sail the sea of sin unruffled, that we may be made tranquil and supported by the Holy Spirit, the unutterable Wisdom, by night and day, unto the perfect day, to sing eternal thanksgiving to the one only Father and Son, Son and Father, Educator and Teacher with the Holy Spirit. All things are for the One, in whom are all things, through whom, being the One, are all things, through whom eternity is, of whom all men are members, to whom is glory, and the ages, whose are all things in their goodness; all things, in their beauty; all things, in their wisdom; all things, in their justice. To him be glory now and forever. Amen.

CLEMENT OF ALEXANDRIA

WE should ask God and the Holy Spirit graciously to dispel every shred of those clouds and vapors, the product of our filthy sins, which with their darkness impede our hearts' vision. Then we shall be able to understand the spirit of his Law and the marvels of it: which was what the prophet meant when he said: "Clear sight be mine, to contemplate the wonders of thy law."

ORIGEN

LET us pray, however, the mercy of the omnipotent God to make us "not only hearers of" his "word," but also "doers" and to bring upon our souls also a flood of his water and destroy in us what he knows should be destroyed and quicken what he knows should be quickened, through Christ our Lord and through his Holy Spirit. To him be glory for ever and ever. Amen.

ORIGEN

BUT may the Lord grant us to believe in the heart, to confess with the mouth, to confirm with works that the convenant of God is in our flesh, that men seeing our good works, might magnify our Father who is in heaven through Jesus Christ our Lord, to whom is glory for ever and ever. Amen.

ORIGEN

JESUS, my feet are dirty. Come and slave for me; pour your water into your basin and come and wash my feet. I am overbold, I know, in asking this, but I dread what you threatened when you said: "If I do not wash your feet, it means you have no companionship with me." Wash my feet, then, because I do want to have companionship with you. And yet, why am I saying: "Wash my feet"? It was all very well for Peter to say that, for in his case all that needed washing was his feet: he was clean through and through. My position is quite different: you may wash me now, but I shall still need that other washing you were thinking of, Lord, when you said: "There is a baptism I must needs be baptized with."

ORIGEN

LET us keep the Scriptures in mind and meditate upon them day and night, persevering in prayer, always on the watch. Let us beg the Lord to give us real knowledge of what we read and to show us not only how to understand it but how to put it into practice, so that we may deserve to obtain spiritual grace, enlightened by the law of the Holy Spirit, through Jesus Christ our Lord, whose power and glory will endure throughout the ages. Amen.

ORIGEN

LET us too stand in the Temple and hold God's Son and embrace him; and that we may deserve leave to withdraw and start on our way toward a better land, let us pray to

God, the all-powerful, and to the little Jesus himself, whom we so much want to speak to and hold in our arms.

His are glory and power now and always. Amen.

ORIGEN

LET us ask the Lord to broaden our ideas, make them clearer, and bring them nearer to the truth, that we may understand the other things too that he has revealed to his prophets. May we study the Holy Spirit's writings under the guidance of the Spirit himself and compare one spiritual interpretation with another, so that our explanation of the texts may be worthy of God and the Holy Spirit, who inspired them. May we do this through Christ Jesus, our Lord, to whom glory and power belong and will belong through all the ages. Amen.

ORIGEN

LET us pray that Jesus may reign over us and that our land may be at peace—that is, that our bodies may be free from the assaults of fleshly desires. When these have ceased, we shall be able to rest, beneath our vines, our fig trees and our olives.

Father, Son, and Holy Spirit will shelter us as we rest, our peace of mind and body once recovered.

Glory to God the eternal, age after age. Amen.

ORIGEN

GREAT is our Lord Jesus, present or absent. To this our gathering and assembly he has given a share of his might. Be it our prayer to the Lord God that each one of us may deserve to receive this. To whom be glory and dominion for ever and ever. Amen.

ORIGEN

O God the Father:
Origin of divinity,
Good beyond all that is good,
Fair beyond all that is fair,
In whom is calmness, peace, concord:

Do thou make up
The dissensions which divide us
From each other,
And bring us back
Into the unity of love,
Which to thy divine nature
May bear some likeness.

As thou art above all things,
Make us one by the unanimity
Of a good mind,
That through the embrace of charity,
And the bonds of godly affection
We spiritually may be one,
As well in ourselves
As in each other,
By that peace of thine
Which maketh all things peaceful:

Through the grace,
The mercy, and the tenderness
Of thine only begotten Son,
Jesus, the Christ, our Lord.

DIONYSIUS OF ALEXANDRIA

LET us pray to the Lord alone without ceasing to ask and, with faith in receiving, straightforward and of one mind, entreating with both groaning and weeping, as those who are placed between the ruins of the moaning and the remains of the fearful, between the manifold destruction of the fallen and the paltry strength of the standing, ought to pray. Let us ask for peace to be restored sooner, to be succored quickly in our hiding places and dangers, for what the Lord deigns to manifest to his servants to be fulfilled: the restoration of his Church, the security of our salvation, serenity after the rains, light after darkness, peaceful calm after storms and dangers, blessed aids of his fatherly love, the accustomed grandeurs of his divine majesty, by which the blasphemy of the persecutors may be beaten back, and the penance of the lapsed may be accomplished, and the strong and stable faith of the persevering may glory. I trust that you, dearly beloved brethren, are always well and mindful of us. Greet the brotherhood in my name and urge them to be mindful of us. Farewell.

CYPRIAN OF CARTHAGE

WE pray and we entreat God, whom those men do not cease to provoke and exasperate, that they may soften their hearts, that they may return to health of mind when this madness has been put aside, that their hearts, filled with the darkness of sin, may recognize the light of repentance, and that they may rather seek that the intercession and prayers of the bishop be poured out for themselves than that they themselves shed the blood of the bishop.

CYPRIAN OF CARTHAGE

FIVE

Prayers from the New Testament Apocrypha

O Word of life, which name I have just given to the tree, I give thee thanks, not with these lips that are nailed fast, nor with the tongue, through which truth and falsehood issues forth, nor with this word that comes forth by the skill of physical nature; but I give thee thanks, O King, with that voice which is known in silence, which is not heard aloud, which does not come forth through the bodily organs, which does not enter the ears of the flesh, that is not heard by corruptible substance, that is not in the world or uttered upon earth, nor is written in books, nor belongs to one but not to another; but with this voice, Jesu Christ, I thank thee, with silence of the voice, with which the spirit within me, that loves thee and speaks to thee and sees thee, makes intercession. Thou art known to the spirit only. Thou art my Father, thou art my Mother, thou art my Brother, thou art Friend, thou art Servant, thou art Housekeeper; thou art the All, and the All is in thee; thou art Being, and there is nothing that is, except thou.

ACTS OF PETER

TO thee, our Lord, be glory and splendor, almighty God, Father of our Lord Jesus Christ. To thee be praise and glory and honor, for ever and ever. Amen. As thou hast fully encouraged and established us now in thee in the sight of all beholders, holy Lord, so strengthen Marcellus and send thy peace to him and his house today; but whatever is lost or astray thou alone canst restore. We all beseech thee, O Lord, the shepherd of sheep that once were scattered, but now shall be gathered in one through thee: receive Marcellus again as one of thy lambs and suffer him no longer to riot in error or in ignorance; but accept him among the number of thy sheep. Even so, Lord, receive him, that with sorrow and tears doth entreat thee.

ACTS OF PETER

O name of the cross, mystery that is concealed! O grace ineffable that is spoken in the name of the cross! O nature of man that cannot be parted from God! O love unspeakable and inseparable, that cannot be disclosed through unclean lips! I seize thee now, being come to the end of my release from here. I will declare thee, what thou art; I will not conceal the mystery of the cross that has long been enclosed and hidden from my soul.

ACTS OF PETER

O God eternal, God of the heavens, God of unutterable majesty, who hast established all things by thy word, who hast broken the chain set fast upon man, who hast brought the light of thy grace to all the world, Father of thine holy Son Jesus Christ, we entreat thee together through thy Son Jesus Christ to strengthen the souls which once were unbelieving but now have faith.

ACTS OF PETER

"MY Lord and my God,
and hope and redeemer,
and leader and guide in all the lands,
be thou with all who serve thee,
and lead me today, since I come to thee!
Let none take my soul,
which I have committed unto thee.
Let not the tax collectors see me,
and let not the exactors lay false charge against me!
Let not the serpent see me,
and let not the children of the dragon hiss me!
Behold, Lord, I have fulfilled thy work
and accomplished thy command.
I have become a slave;
therefore today do I receive freedom.
Do thou now give it to me completely!
But this I say not as one doubting,
but that they may hear who ought to hear."

ACTS OF THOMAS

JESUS, the hidden mystery that has been revealed to us, thou art he who has made known to us many mysteries; who did set me apart from all my companions and speak to me three words wherewith I am inflamed, and tell them to others I cannot; Jesus, man, slain, corpse, buried; Jesus, God of God, Saviour who dost quicken the dead and heal the sick; Jesus, who wert in need like a poor man, and dost save as one who has no need; thou who didst catch the fish for the breakfast and the dinner, and didst make all satisfied with a little bread; Jesus, who didst rest from the weariness of the journey like a man, and walk upon the waves like a God; Jesus most high, voice arising like the sun from the perfect mercy, Saviour of all, right hand of the light which overthrows the Evil One by his own nature, thou who dost gather all his nature into one place; thou of many forms, who art only begotten, the firstborn of many brethren; God from God Most High, man despised until now; Jesus Christ, who dost not neglect us when we call upon thee; who art become an occasion of life to all mankind; who for our sakes wast judged and shut up in prison, and dost set free all that are in bonds; who wast called a deceiver, and dost deliver thine own from deception; I pray thee for these who stand here and believe in thee. For they crave to obtain thy gifts, having good hope in thy help, and having their refuge in thy greatness. They have their ears open to hear from us the words which are spoken to them. Let thy peace come and dwell in them, and let it renew them from their former deeds, and let them put off the old man with his deeds and put on the new who is now proclaimed to them by me.

ACTS OF THOMAS

I praise thee, Lord Jesus, that thou hast revealed thy truth in these men. For thou alone art the God of truth, and no other; and thou art he who knows all that is unknown to the many; thou, Lord, art he who in all things shows mercy and forbearance to men. For men because of the error that is in them forsook thee, but thou didst not forsake them. And now as I beseech and supplicate thee, receive the king and his brother and unite them with thy flock, cleansing them with thy washing and anointing them with thy oil from the error which surrounds them. Preserve them also from the wolves, leading them in thy pastures. Give them to drink from thine ambrosial spring which neither is turbid nor dries up. For they pray thee and implore and desire to become thy ministers and servants, and for this cause they are content even to be persecuted by thine enemies, and for thy sake to be hated by them and be despitefully used and put to death, even as thou for our sakes didst suffer all these things that thou mightest preserve us, who art Lord and truly a good Shepherd. But do thou grant to them that they may have confidence in thee alone, and [obtain] the help which cometh from thee and hope of their salvation, which they expect from thee alone, and that they may be established in thy mysteries and receive of thy graces and gifts the perfect good, and may flourish in thy service, and bring forth fruit to perfection in thy Father.

ACTS OF THOMAS

O God exceeding great and all-wise, King of the ages, indescribable, ineffable, who didst create the breadths of the heavens by thy word and arrange the vault of Heaven in harmony, who didst give form to disorderly matter and didst bring together that which was separated, who didst part the gloom of the darkness from the light, who didst make the waters to flow from the same source, before whom the beings of the air tremble and the creatures of the earth fear, who didst give to the earth its place and didst not wish it to perish, in bestowing upon it abundant rain and caring for the nourishment of all things, the eternal Word (*Logos*) of the Father. The seven heavens could scarcely contain thee, but thou wast pleased to be contained in me, without causing me pain, thou who art the perfect Word (*Logos*) of the Father, through whom everything was created. Glorify thine exceedingly great name, and allow me to speak before thy holy apostles.

GOSPEL OF BARTHOLOMEW, PRAYER OF MARY

O thou that didst choose us for the apostolate among the Gentiles; O God who has sent us into all the world; who hast shown thyself through the law and the prophets; who hast never rested, but from the foundation of the world dost always save those who can be saved; who hast revealed thyself through all nature; who hast proclaimed thyself even among beasts; who hast made even the lonely and embittered soul grow tame and quiet; who hast given thyself to it when it thirsted for thy words; who hast speedily appeared to it when it was dying; who hast shown thyself to it as a law when sunk into lawlessness; who has revealed thyself to it when overcome by Satan; who hast overcome its adversary when it took refuge with thee; who hast given to it thine hand and aroused it from the works of Hades; who hast not suffered it to conform to the body; who hast shown it its own enemy; who hast made for it a pure knowledge of thee, O God Jesu; Father of beings beyond the heavens, Lord of those that are in the heavens, Law of the ethereal beings and Path of those in the air; Guardian of beings upon earth, and Terror of those beneath the earth, and Grace of those that are thine; receive also the soul of thy John which, it may be, is approved by thee.

Thou who hast kept me also till this present hour pure for thyself and untouched by union with a woman; who when I wished to marry in my youth didst appear to me and say to me, "John, I need thee"; who didst prepare for me also an infirmity of the body; who on the third occasion when I wished to marry didst prevent me at once, and then at the third hour of the day didst say to me upon the sea, "John, if thou wert not mine, I should have allowed thee to marry"; who didst blind me for two years, letting me be grieved and entreat thee; who in the third year didst open the eyes of my understanding and didst give me back my eyes that are seen; who when I regained my sight didst disclose to me the repugnance even of looking closely at a woman; who hast saved me from the illusion of the present and guided me into that life which endureth forever; who hast rid me of the foul madness that is in the flesh; who hast snatched me from a bitter death and presented me only to thee; who hast silenced the secret disease of my soul and cut off the open deed; who hast weakened and expelled the rebellious enemy within me; who hast made my love for thee unsullied; who hast ruled my course to thee unbroken; who hast given me faith in thee undoubting; who hast instructed my knowledge of thee with purity; who givest to each man's works their due reward; who hast inspired my soul to have no possession but thee alone—for what is more precious than thee? So, Lord, now that I have fulfilled the charge which I was entrusted by thee count me worthy of thy rest and grant me my end in thee, which is inexpressible and unutterable salvation.

And as I come to thee let the fire retreat and the darkness yield, let chaos be enfeebled, the furnace grow dim and Gehenna be quenched; let angels follow and demons be afraid, let the rulers be shattered and the powers fall; let the places on the right hand stand fast and those on the left be removed; let the Devil be silenced, let Satan be derided, let his wrath be burned out, let his madness be calmed, let his vengeance be disgraced, let his assault be distressed, let his children be wounded and all his root be uprooted. And grant me to finish my way to thee preserved from violence and insult, receiving what thou hast promised to them that live purely and love thee alone.

And having sealed himself in every part, standing thus, he said "Be thou with me, Lord Jesus Christ"; and he lay down in the trench where he had spread out his clothes; and he said to us, "Peace be with you, my brethren," and gave up his spirit rejoicing.

ACTS OF JOHN

O Jesus, who hast woven this crown with thy weaving, who has united these many flowers into the unfading flower of thy countenance, who hast sown these words in my heart; thou only Protector of thy servants, and Physician who healest for naught; only Doer of good and despiser of none, only Merciful and Lover of men, only Saviour and Righteous One; who ever seest the deeds of all and dwellest in all and art everywhere present, encompassing all things and filling all things; Christ Jesu, God, Lord, that with thy gifts and thy mercy protectest those that hope in thee, who exactly knowest all the devices and the malice of him that is everywhere our adversary, which he contriveth against us; do thou only, O Lord, assist thy servants by thy visitation. Even so, Lord!

ACTS OF JOHN

GRACE to you and peace from God the Father and the Lord Jesus Christ. I thank Christ in all my prayers that you are steadfast in him and persevering in his works, in expectation of the promise for the day of judgment. And may you not be deceived by the vain talk of some people who tell [you] tales that they may lead you away from the truth of the Gospel which is proclaimed by me. And now may God grant that those who come from me for the furtherance of the truth of the Gospel may be able to serve and to do good works for the well-being of eternal life. And now my bonds are manifest, which I suffer in Christ, on account of which I am glad and rejoice. This ministers to me unto eternal salvation, which itself is effected through your prayers and by the help of the Holy Spirit, whether it be through life or through death. For my life is in Christ and to die is joy to me. And this will his mercy work in you, that you may have the same love and be of one mind. Therefore, beloved, as you have heard in my presence, so hold fast and do in the fear of God, and eternal life will be your portion. For it is God who works in you. And do without hesitation what you do. And for the rest, beloved, rejoice in Christ and beware of those who are out for sordid gain. May all your requests be manifest before God, and be ye steadfast in the mind of Christ. And what is pure, true, proper, just, and lovely, do. And what you have heard and received, hold in your heart and peace will be with you. Salute all the brethren with the holy kiss. The saints salute you. The grace of the Lord Jesus Christ be with your spirit.

PAUL'S EPISTLE TO THE LAODICEANS

SIX

The Earliest Liturgical Prayers

BUT we, after we have thus washed him who has been convinced and has assented to our teaching, bring him to the place where those who are called brethren are assembled, in order that we may offer hearty prayers in common for ourselves and for the baptized illuminated person, and for all others in every place, that we may be counted worthy, now that we have learned the truth, by our works also to be found good citizens and keepers of the commandments, so that we may be saved with an everlasting salvation. Having ended the prayers, we salute one another with a kiss. There is then brought to the president of the brethren bread and a cup of wine mixed with water; and he taking them, gives praise and glory to the Father of the universe, through the name of the Son and of the Holy Ghost, and offers thanks at considerable length for our being counted worthy to receive these things at his hands. And when he has concluded the prayers and thanksgivings, all the people present express their assent by saying Amen. This word Amen answers in the Hebrew language to so be it. And when the president has given thanks, and all the people have expressed their assent, those who are called by us deacons give to each of those present to partake of the bread and wine mixed with water over which the thanksgiving was pronounced, and to those who are absent they carry away a portion.

And this food is called among us the Eucharist, of which no one is allowed to partake but the man who believes that the things which we teach are true, and who has been washed with the washing that is for the remission of sins, and unto regeneration, and who is so living as Christ has enjoined. For not as common bread and common drink do we receive these; but in like manner as Jesus Christ our Saviour, having been made flesh by the Word of God, had both flesh and blood for our salvation, so likewise have we been taught that the food which is blessed by the prayer of his word, and from which our blood and flesh by transmutation are nourished, is the flesh and blood of that Jesus who was made flesh. For the apostles, in the memoirs composed by them, which are called Gospels, have thus delivered unto us what was enjoined upon them; that Jesus took bread, and when he had given thanks, said, "This do ye in remembrance of me, this is my body"; and that, after the same manner, having taken the cup and given thanks, he said, "This is my blood"; and gave it to them alone. Which the wicked devils have imitated in the mysteries of Mithras, commanding the same thing to be done. For, that bread and a cup of water are placed with certain incantations in the mystic rites of one who is being initiated, you either know or can learn.

And we afterwards continually remind each other of these things. And the wealthy among us help the needy; and we always keep together; and for all things wherewith we are supplied, we bless the Maker of all through his Son Jesus Christ, and through the Holy Ghost. And on the day called Sunday, all who live in cities or in the country gather together to one place, and the memoirs of the apostles or the writings of the prophets are read, as long as time permits; then, when the reader has ceased, the president verbally instructs, and exhorts to the imitation of these good things. Then we all rise together and pray, and, as we before said, when our prayer is ended, bread and wine and water are brought, and the president in like manner offers prayers and thanksgivings, according to his ability, and the people assent, saying Amen; and there is a distribution to each, and a participation of that over which thanks have been given, and to those who are absent a portion is sent by the deacons. And they who are well to do, and willing, give what each thinks fit; and what is collected is deposited with the president, who succors the orphans and widows, and those who, through sickness or any other cause, are in want, and those who are in bonds, and the strangers sojourning among us, and in a word takes care of all who are in need. But Sunday is the day on which we all hold our common assembly, because it is the first day on which God, having wrought a change in the darkness and matter, made the world; and Jesus Christ our Saviour on the same day rose from the dead. For he was crucified on the day before that of Saturn (Saturday); and on the day after that of Saturn, which is the day of the Sun, having appeared to his apostles and disciples, he taught them these things, which we have submitted to you also for your consideration.

JUSTIN MARTYR

REGARDING the Eucharist. Give thanks as follows: First, concerning the cup:

We give thee thanks, our Father, for the holy vine of David thy servant, which thou hast made known to us through Jesus, thy Servant. To thee be the glory for evermore.

NEXT, concerning the broken bread:

We give thee thanks, our Father, for the life and knowledge which thou hast made known to us through Jesus, thy Servant. To thee be the glory for evermore.

As this broken bread was scattered over the hills and then, when gathered, became one mass, so may thy Church be gathered from the ends of the earth into thy Kingdom. For thine is the glory and the power through Jesus Christ for evermore.

LET no one eat and drink of your Eucharist but those baptized in the name of the Lord; to this, too, the saying of the Lord is applicable: Do not give to dogs what is sacred.

After you have taken your fill of food, give thanks as follows:

We give thee thanks, O Holy Father, for thy holy name which thou hast enshrined in our hearts, and for the knowledge and faith and immortality which thou hast made known to us through Jesus, thy Servant. To thee be the glory for evermore.

Thou, Lord Almighty, hast created all things for the sake of thy name and hast given food and drink for men to enjoy, that they may give thanks to thee; but to us thou hast vouchsafed spiritual food and drink and eternal life through Jesus, thy Servant. Above all, we give thee thanks because thou art mighty. To thee be the glory for evermore.

Remember, O Lord, thy Church: deliver her from all evil, perfect her in thy love, and from the winds assemble her, the sanctified, in thy kingdom which thou hast prepared for her.
For thine is the power and the glory for evermore.

May grace come, and this world pass away!
Hosanna to the God of David!
If anyone is holy, let him advance; if anyone is not, let him be converted. Marana tha!
Amen.

THE DIDACHE

WE render thanks unto thee, O God, through thy beloved Servant Jesus Christ, whom in the last times thou didst send [to be] a Saviour and Redeemer and the Angel of thy counsel; who is thy Word inseparable from thee; through whom thou madest all things and in whom thou wast well pleased; whom thou didst send from Heaven into the Virgin's womb, and who conceived within her was made flesh, and demonstrated to be thy Son, being born of Holy Spirit and a Virgin; who fulfilling thy will and procuring for thee a holy people, stretched forth his hands for suffering (*or* for the passion) that he might release from sufferings them who have believed in thee; who when he was betrayed to voluntary suffering (*or* the passion) in order that he might abolish death and rend the bonds of the devil and tread down Hell and enlighten the righteous and establish the ordinance and demonstrate the resurrection, taking bread and making Eucharist to thee, said: Take, eat; this is my body, which is *or* will be broken for you.

Likewise also the cup, saying: This is my blood which is shed for you.

When ye do this ye do (*or* make ye) my "anamnesis."

Now, therefore, doing the "anamnesis" of his death and resurrection we offer to thee the bread and cup making Eucharist to thee because thou hast made us worthy to stand before thee and minister as priests to thee.

And we pray thee that thou wouldest grant to all who partake to be made one, that they may be fulfilled with the Holy Spirit for the confirmation of their faith in truth; that we may praise and glorify thee through thy Servant Jesus Christ through whom honor and glory be unto thee with the Holy Spirit in thy holy Church, now and forever and world without end.

APOSTOLIC TRADITION OF HIPPOLYTUS

LET us pray for peace, which is Heaven's gift. May the Lord in his mercy give us peace.

Let us pray for faith. May the Lord give us grace to keep our faith in him untainted to the end.

Let us pray for unity of hearts and minds. May the Lord keep our minds and hearts as one.

Let us pray for patience. In all our afflictions may the Lord grant us patience to the end.

Let us pray for the apostles. May the Lord make us please him as they pleased him; may he fit us to receive the inheritance they have received.

Let us pray for the holy prophets. May the Lord add us to their number.

Let us pray for the holy confessors. The Lord grant that we may end our lives in the same frame of mind as they did.

Let us pray for the bishop. May our Lord grant him a long life and keep him true to the faith, that breaking the bread of truth as he ought, he may preside over the Church blamelessly and without reproach.

Let us pray for priests. May God not take the spirit of the priesthood from them, but grant them zeal and piety to the end.

Let us pray for deacons. The Lord grant that they may stay the course and attain holiness; and may he bear their labors and their charity in mind.

Let us pray for deaconesses. May the Lord answer their prayers and fill their hearts with all spiritual blessings and support them in their labors.

Let us pray for subdeacons and lectors. May the Lord give them patience and reward them for it.

Let us pray for the faithful throughout the world. The Lord grant that they may keep the faith whole and entire.

Let us pray for the empire. May the Lord grant it peace.

Let us pray for princes. The Lord grant that they may know him and fear him.
Let us pray for the whole world. May the Lord provide for all creatures and give to each what is best for it.

LITURGICAL FRAGMENT

ALL-POWERFUL Lord, God of our fathers Abraham, Isaac, and Jacob and of the just among their descendants: you made Heaven and earth and all the splendor of them, chained up the sea with one word of command, closed the abyss and sealed it with your dread and glorious name. The whole creation fears you and trembles at your power, because your glory is too great for it to bear, and sinners cannot face the anger in your threats.

But the mercy behind your promise is boundless and unfathomable; you are the Lord most high, long-suffering, patient, easily forgiving men their sins.

Of your great kindness, Lord, you promised to forgive those who were sorry they had sinned against you; of your great mercy, you declared that sinners should be saved by repentance. You did not decree that Abraham, Isaac, and Jacob should repent, for they were just and had not sinned against you; but you do prescribe repentance for me, because I am a sinner—my sins, indeed, are more numerous than the grains of sand on the seashore. I have fallen so often, Lord, and I am not fit to raise my eyes to Heaven because I have so many sins on my conscience.

The weight of the iron chains that bind me bows me down, so that I cannot lift up my head; I dare not even breathe, because I have provoked your anger and done evil in your presence. I have not done what you wanted me to do, I have not carried out your orders; I have done wrong and offended you over and over again.

And now I bend my knees before you and bend my heart to you as well. I appeal to your kindness. I have sinned, Lord, I have sinned; I admit my baseness.

I beg you, Lord, forgive me; forgive me, and do not destroy me as well as my sins. Do not be angry with me forever or condemn me and cast me into the depths of the earth.

You are indeed the God of the repentant. Your treatment of me shows how kind you are: in your great mercy, you would save even such a wretch as I.

I will sing your praises all the days of my life, like the armies of Heaven, which never cease to acclaim your greatness.

Glory to you throughout the ages. Amen.

THE PRAYER OF MANASSES, DIDASCALIA

GREAT art thou, O Lord Almighty, and great is thy power, and of thy understanding there is no number. Our Creator and Saviour, rich in benefits, long-suffering, and the bestower of mercy, who dost not take away thy salvation from thy creatures: for thou art good by nature, and sparest sinners, and invitest them to repentance; for admonition is the effect of thy bowels of compassion. For how should we abide if we were required to come to judgment immediately, when, after so much long-suffering, we hardly get clear of our miserable condition? The heavens declare thy dominion, and the earth shakes with earthquakes, and hanging upon nothing, declares thy unshaken steadfastness. The sea raging with waves, and feeding a flock of ten thousand creatures, is bounded with sand, as standing in awe at thy command, and compels all men to cry out: "How great are thy works, O Lord! in wisdom hast thou made them all: the earth is full of thy creation." And the bright host of angels and the intellectual spirits say to Palmoni, "There is but one holy Being"; and the holy seraphim, together with the six-winged cherubim, who sing to thee their triumphal song, cry out with never-ceasing voices, "Holy, holy, holy, Lord God of hosts! heaven and earth are full of thy glory"; and the other multitudes of the orders, angels, archangels, thrones, dominions, principalities, authorities, and powers cry aloud, and say, "Blessed be the glory of the Lord out of his place." But Israel, thy Church on earth, taken out of the Gentiles, emulating the heavenly powers night and day, with a full heart and a willing soul sings, "The chariot of God is ten thousandfold thousands of them that rejoice: the Lord is among them in Sinai, in the holy place." The Heaven knows him who fixed it as a cube of stone, in the form of an arch, upon nothing, who united the land and water to one another, and scattered the vital air all abroad, and conjoined fire therewith for warmth, and the comfort against darkness. The choir of stars strikes us with admiration, declaring him that numbers them, and showing him that names them; the animals declare him that puts life into them; the trees show him that makes them grow: all which creatures, being made by thy word, show forth the greatness of thy power. Wherefore every man ought to send up a hymn from his very soul to thee, through Christ, in the name of all the rest, since he has power over them all by thy appointment. For thou art kind in thy benefits, and beneficent in thy bowels of compassion, who alone art almighty: for when thou willest, to be able is present with thee; for thy eternal power both quenches flame, and stops the mouths of lions, and tames whales, and raises up the sick, and overrules the power of all things, and overturns the host of enemies, and casts down a people numbered in their arrogance. Thou art he who art in Heaven, he who art on earth, he who art in the sea, he who art in finite things, thyself unconfined by anything. For of thy majesty there is no boundary; for it is not ours, O Lord, but the oracle of thy servant, who said, "And thou shalt know in thine heart that the Lord thy God he is God in Heaven above, and on earth beneath, and there is none other besides thee": for there is no God besides thee alone, there is none holy besides thee, the Lord, the God of knowledge, the God of the saints, holy above all holy beings; for they are sanctified by thy hands. Thou art glorious, and highly exalted, invisible by nature, and unsearchable in thy judgments; whose life is without want, whose duration can never alter or fail, whose operation is without toil, whose greatness is unlimited, whose excellency is perpetual, whose habitation is inaccessible, whose dwelling is unchangeable, whose knowledge is without beginning, whose truth is immutable, whose work is without assistants, whose dominion cannot be taken away, whose monarchy is without succession, whose kingdom is without end, whose strength is irresistible, whose army is very numerous: for thou art the Father of wisdom, the Creator of the creation, by a Mediator, as the cause; the Bestower of providence, the Giver of laws, the Supplier of want, the Punisher of the ungodly, and the Rewarder of the righteous; the God and Father of Christ, and the Lord of those that are pious toward him, whose promise is infallible, whose judgment is without bribes, whose sentiments are immutable, whose piety is incessant, whose thanksgiving is everlasting, through whom adoration is worthily due to thee from every rational and holy nature.

APOSTOLIC CONSTITUTIONS

LET us pray for the peace and happy settlement of the world, and of the holy churches; that the God of the whole world may afford us his everlasting peace, and such as may not be taken away from us; that he may preserve us in a full prosecution of such virtue as is according to godliness.

Let us pray for our enemies, and those that hate us. Let us pray for those that persecute us for the name of the Lord, that the Lord may pacify their anger, and scatter their wrath against us.

Save us, and raise us up, O God, by thy mercy. Let us rise up, and let us pray earnestly, and dedicate ourselves and one another to the living God, through his Christ.

APOSTOLIC CONSTITUTIONS

LET us pray for our brethren that are at rest in Christ, that God, the Lover of mankind, who has received his soul, may forgive him every sin, voluntary and involuntary, and may be merciful and gracious to him, and give him his lot in the land of the pious that are sent into the bosom of Abraham and Isaac and Jacob, with all those that have pleased him and done his will from the beginning of the world, whence all sorrow, grief, and lamentation are banished. Let us arise, let us dedicate ourselves and one another to the eternal God, through that Word which was in the beginning.

APOSTOLIC CONSTITUTIONS

SAVE us, O God, and raise us up by thy Christ. Let us stand up, and beg for the mercies of the Lord, and his compassions, for the angel of peace, for what things are good and profitable, for a Christian departure out of this life, an evening and a night of peace, and free from sin; and let us beg that the whole course of our life may be unblamable. Let us dedicate ourselves and one another to the living God through his Christ.

APOSTOLIC CONSTITUTIONS

O God, the God of spirits and of all flesh, who art beyond compare, and standest in need of nothing, who hast given the sun to have rule over the day, and the moon and the stars to have rule over the night, do thou now also look down upon us with gracious eyes, and receive our morning thanksgivings, and have mercy upon us; for we have not "spread out our hands unto a strange God"; for there is not among us any new God, but thou, the eternal God, who art without end, who hast given us our being through Christ, and given us our well-being through him. Do thou vouchsafe us also, through him, eternal life; with whom glory and honor and worship be to thee and to the Holy Spirit forever. Amen.

APOSTOLIC CONSTITUTIONS

O God, who art without beginning and without end, the Maker of the whole world by Christ, and the Provider for it, but before all his God and Father, the Lord of the Spirit, and the King of intelligible and sensible beings; who hast made the day for the works of light, and the night for the refreshment of our infirmity—for "the day is thine, the night also is thine: thou hast prepared the light and the sun"—do thou now, O Lord, thou lover of mankind, and Fountain of all good, mercifully accept of this our evening thanksgiving. Thou who hast brought us through the length of the day, and hast brought us to the beginnings of the night, preserve us by thy Christ, afford us a peaceable evening, and a night free from sin, and vouchsafe us everlasting life by thy Christ, through whom glory, honor, and worship be to thee in the Holy Spirit forever. Amen.

APOSTOLIC CONSTITUTIONS

THOU, who hast bound the strong man, and spoiled all that was in his house, who hast given us power over serpents and scorpions to tread upon them, and upon all the power of the enemy; who hast delivered the serpent, that murderer of men, bound to us, as a sparrow to children, whom all things dread, and tremble before the face of thy power; who hast cast him down as lightning from Heaven to earth, not with a fall from a place, but from honor to dishonor, on account of his voluntary evil disposition; whose look dries the abysses, and threatening melts the mountains, and whose truth remains forever; whom the infants praise, and sucking babes bless; whom angels sing hymns to, and adore; who lookest upon the earth, and makest it tremble; who touchest the mountains, and they smoke; who threatenest the sea, and driest it up, and makest all its rivers as desert, and the clouds are the dust of his feet; who walkest upon the sea as upon the firm ground;

thou only begotten God, the Son of the great Father, rebuke these wicked spirits, and deliver the works of thy hands from the power of the adverse spirit. For to thee is due glory, honor, and worship, and by thee to thy Father, in the Holy Spirit, forever. Amen.

APOSTOLIC CONSTITUTIONS

OUR eternal Saviour, the King of gods, who alone art almighty, and the Lord, the God of all beings, and the God of our holy and blameless fathers, and of those before us; the God of Abraham, and of Isaac, and of Jacob; who art merciful and compassionate, long-suffering, and abundant in mercy; to whom every heart is naked, and by whom every heart is seen, and to whom every secret thought is revealed: to thee do the souls of the righteous cry aloud, upon thee do the hopes of the godly trust, thou Father of the blameless, thou hearer of the supplication of those that call upon thee with uprightness, and who knowest the supplications that are not uttered: for thy providence reaches as far as the inmost parts of mankind; and by thy knowledge thou searchest the thoughts of every one, and in every region of the whole earth the incense of prayer and supplication is sent up to thee. O thou who hast appointed this present world as a place of combat to righteousness, and hast opened to all the gate of mercy, and hast demonstrated to every man by implanted knowledge, and natural judgment, and the admonitions of the law, how the possession of riches is not everlasting, the ornament of beauty is not perpetual, our strength and force are easily dissolved; and that all is vapor and vanity; and that only the good conscience of faith unfeigned passes through the midst of the heavens, and returning with truth, takes hold of the right hand of the joy which is to come. And withal, before the promise of the restoration of all things is accomplished, the soul itself exults in hope, and is joyful. For from that truth which was in our forefather, Abraham, when he changed his way thou didst guide him by a vision, and didst teach him what kind of state this world is; and knowledge went before his faith, and faith was the consequence of his knowledge; and the covenant did follow after his faith. For thou saidst: "I will make thy seed as the stars of Heaven, and as the sand which is by the seashore." Moreover, when thou hadst given him Isaac, and knewest him to be like him in his mode of life, thou wast then called his God, saying: "I will be a God to thee, and to thy seed after thee." And when our father Jacob was sent into Mesopotamia, thou showedst him Christ, and by him speakest, saying: "Behold, I am with thee, and I will increase thee, and multiply thee exceedingly." And so spakest thou to Moses, thy faithful and holy servant, at the vision of the bush: "I am he that is; this is my name forever, and my memorial for generations of generations." O thou great protector of the posterity of Abraham, thou art blessed forever.

APOSTOLIC CONSTITUTIONS

WE beseech thee, the Father of the only-begotten, the Lord of the universe, the Artificer of the creatures, the Maker of things that have been made; clean hands do we stretch out, and our thoughts do we unfold to thee, O Lord. We pray thee, have compassion, spare, benefit, improve, multiply us in virtue and faith and knowledge. Visit us, O Lord; to thee we display our own weaknesses. Be propitious and have pity on us all in common. Have pity, benefit this people. Make it gentle and sober-minded and clean; and send angelic powers, in order that all this thy people may be holy and reverend. I beseech thee send Holy Spirit into our mind and give us grace to learn the divine Scriptures from the Holy Spirit, and to interpret, cleanly and worthily, that all the lay people present may be helped, through thy only-begotten Jesus Christ in Holy Spirit, through whom to thee is the glory and the strength both now and to all the ages of the ages. Amen.

EUCHOLOGIUM OF SERAPION

IT is meet and right to praise, to hymn, to glorify thee the uncreated Father of the only-begotten Jesus Christ. We praise thee, O uncreated God, who art unsearchable, ineffable, incomprehensible by any created substance. We praise thee who art known of thy Son, the only-begotten, who through him art spoken of and interpreted and made known to created nature. We praise thee who knowest the Son and revealest to the saints the glories that are about him: who art known of thy begotten Word, and art brought to the sight and interpreted to the understanding of the saints. We praise thee, O unseen Father, Provider of immortality. Thou art the Fount of life, the Fount of light, the Fount of all grace and all truth, O Lover of men, O Lover of the poor, who reconcilest thyself to all, and drawest all to thyself through the advent of thy beloved Son. We beseech thee make us living men. Give us a spirit of light, that "we may know thee the true God and him whom thou didst send, even Jesus Christ." Give us Holy Spirit, that we may be able to tell forth and to enunciate thy unspeakable mysteries. May the Lord Jesus speak in us and Holy Spirit, and hymn thee through us.

For thou art "far above all rule and authority and power and dominion, and every name that is named, not only in this world but also in that which is to come." Beside thee stand thousand thousands and myriad myriads of angels, archangels, thrones, dominions, principalities, powers: by thee stand the two most honorable six-winged seraphim, with two wings covering the face, and with two the feet, and with two flying and crying holy, with whom receive also our cry of "holy" as we say: Holy, holy, holy, Lord of Sabaoth, full is the Heaven and the earth of thy glory.

Full is the Heaven, full also is the earth of thy excellent glory. Lord of Hosts, fill also this sacrifice with thy power and thy participation: for to thee have we offered this living sacrifice, this bloodless oblation. To thee we have offered this bread the likeness of the body of the Only-begotten. This bread is the likeness of the holy body, because the Lord Jesus Christ in the night in which he was betrayed took bread and broke and gave to his disciples saying, "Take ye and eat, this is my body which is being broken for you for remission of sins." Wherefore we also making the likeness of the death have offered the bread, and beseech thee through this sacrifice, be reconciled to all of us and be merciful, O God of truth: and as this bread had been scattered on the top of the mountains and gathered together came to be one, so also gather thy holy Church out of every nation and every country and every city and village and house and make one living catholic Church. We have offered also the cup, the likeness of the blood, because the Lord Jesus Christ, taking a cup after supper, said to his own disciples, "Take ye, drink, this is the new covenant, which is my blood, which is being shed for you for remission of sins." Wherefore we have also offered the cup, presenting a likeness of the blood.

O God of truth, let thy holy Word come upon this bread that the bread may become body of the Word, and upon this cup that the cup may become blood of the Truth; and make all who communicate to receive a medicine of life for the healing of every sickness and for the strengthening of all advancement and virtue, not for condemnation, O God of truth, and not for censure and reproach. For we have invoked thee, the uncreated, through the Only-begotten in Holy Spirit.

Let this people receive mercy, let it be counted worthy of advancement, let angels be sent forth as companions to the people for bringing to naught of the Evil One and for establishment of the Church.

We intercede also on behalf of all who have been laid to rest, whose memorial we are making. *After the recitation of the names:* Sanctify these souls: for thou knowest all. Sanctify all souls laid to rest in the Lord. And number them with all thy holy powers and give to them a place and a mansion in thy kingdom.

Receive also the thanksgiving (Eucharist) of the people, and bless those who have offered the offerings and the thanksgivings, and grant health and soundness and cheerfulness and all advancement of soul and body to this whole people through the only-begotten Jesus Christ in Holy Spirit; as it was and is and shall be to generations of generations and to all the ages of the ages. Amen.

Count us worthy of this communion also, O God of truth, and make our bodies to contain purity and our souls prudence and knowledge. And make us wise, O God of compassions, by the participation of the body and the blood, because through thy Only-begotten to thee is the glory and the strength in Holy Spirit, now and to all the ages of the ages. Amen.

I stretch out the hand upon this people and pray that the hand of the truth may be stretched out and blessing given to this people on account of thy loving kindness, O God of compassions, and the mysteries that are present. May a hand of piety and power and sound discipline and cleanness and all holiness bless this people, and continually preserve it to advancement and improvement through thy only-begotten Jesus Christ in Holy Spirit both now and to all the ages of the ages. Amen.

We thank thee, Master, that thou hast called those who have erred, and hast taken to thy self those who have sinned, and hast set aside the threat that was against us, giving indulgence by thy loving kindness, and wiping it away by repentance, and casting it off by the knowledge that regards thyself. We give thanks to thee, that thou hast given us communion of the body and blood. Bless us, bless this people, make us to have a part with the body and the blood through thy only-begotten Son, through whom to thee is the glory and the strength in Holy Spirit both now and ever and to all the ages of the ages. Amen.

We bless through the name of thy only-begotten Jesus Christ these creatures, we name the name of him who suffered, who was crucified, and rose again, and who sitteth on the right hand of the uncreated, upon this water and upon this oil. Grant healing power upon these creatures that every fever and every evil spirit and every sickness may depart through the drinking and the anointing, and that the partaking of these creatures may be a healing medicine, and a medicine of soundness, in the name of thy only-begotten Jesus Christ, through whom to thee is the glory and the strength in Holy Spirit to all the ages of the ages. Amen.

O loving God of truth, let the communion of the body and the blood go along with this people. Let their bodies be living bodies, and their souls be clean souls. Grant this blessing to be a keeping of their communion, and a security to the Eucharist that has been celebrated: and make blessed all of them in common and make them elect through thy only-begotten Jesus Christ in Holy Spirit both now and to all the ages of the ages. Amen.

EUCHOLOGIUM OF SERAPION

WE may make full confession to thee, O God who lovest man, and throw before thee our weaknesses, and beseech thee that strength may be imparted to us. Pardon our foregone sins and remit all our faults that have passed by and make us new men. Render us all servants of thine own and clean. To thee we dedicate ourselves; receive us, O God of truth.

Receive this people, grant that it may be entirely thine own. Grant it entirely to walk unblamably and cleanly. Let them be joined in symmetry with the heavenly ones; let them be numbered together with the angels; let them become entirely elect and holy.

We beseech thee on behalf of those who have believed and have come to full knowledge of the Lord Jesus Christ; let them be confirmed in the faith, and in the knowledge and in the doctrine.

We pray thee on behalf of all this people, be reconciled to all, make thyself known. Reveal thy bright light; let all know thee the uncreated Father and thy only-begotten Son Jesus Christ.

We pray for all rulers, may they have a peaceable life.

We pray for the rest of the catholic Church.

We pray thee, O God of compassions, for freemen and slaves, males and women, old men and children, poor and rich; display to all thine own special good, and stretch forth on all thine own special loving kindness; have compassion on all and grant to all to turn to thee.

We beseech thee for those who are traveling from home, grant them an angel of peace as their fellow traveler, that they may receive no hurt from anyone, that they may finish their voyage and their travels in much cheerfulness.

We beseech thee for those who are afflicted and in bonds and in poverty; give rest to each, free them from bonds, bringing them out of poverty; comfort all, thou who art the Comforter and Consoler.

We pray for the sick, grant them health and raise them

up from their sickness, and make them to have perfect health of body and soul: for thou art the Saviour and Benefactor, thou art the Lord and King of all.

We have besought thee on behalf of all through thy only-begotten Jesus Christ, through whom to thee is the glory and the strength in Holy Spirit both now and to all the ages of the ages. Amen.

EUCHOLOGIUM OF SERAPION

GOD, who hast authority of life and death, God of the spirits and Master of all flesh, God who killest and makest alive, who bringest down to the gates of Hades and bringest up, who createst the spirit of man within him and takest to thyself the souls of the saints and givest rest, who alterest and changest and transformest thy creatures, as is right and expedient, being thyself alone incorruptible, unalterable and eternal, we beseech thee for the repose and rest of this thy servant or this thine handmaiden: give rest to his soul, his spirit, in green places, in chambers of rest with Abraham and Isaac and Jacob and all thy saints: and raise up his body in the day which thou hast ordained, according to thy promises which cannot lie, that thou mayest render to it also the heritage of which it is worthy in thy holy pastures. Remember not his transgressions and sins: and cause his going forth to be peaceable and blessed. Heal the griefs of those that pertain to him with the spirit of consolation, and grant unto us all a good end through thy only-begotten Jesus Christ, through whom to thee is the glory and the strength in Holy Spirit to the ages of the ages. Amen.

EUCHOLOGIUM OF SERAPION

O Lord, All-Sovereign, seal the adhesion of this thy servant which has now been made to thee, and continually keep his character and his manner of life unchangeable, that he may no longer minister to those that are worse, but may worship in the God of truth, and serve thee, the Maker of all things, to the end that he may be rendered perfect and thine own through thy only-begotten Jesus Christ, through whom to thee is the glory and the strength in Holy Spirit both now and to all the ages of the ages. Amen.

EUCHOLOGIUM OF SERAPION

WE beseech thee, the Overlooker and Lord and Fashioner of the body and Maker of the soul, thee who didst fit together man, thee who art the Steward and Governor of the whole race of men, thee who art reconciled and made gentle because of thine own love of men: be propitious, Master: assist and heal all that are sick. Rebuke the sicknesses: raise up those that are lying down: give glory to thy holy name and to that of thy only-begotten Jesus Christ, through whom to thee is the glory and the strength in Holy Spirit, both now and to all the ages of the ages. Amen.

EUCHOLOGIUM OF SERAPION

FROM all eternity, O Jesus Christ, you have been our Lord and our God: so did the Father will it. Yet in this, the last of all periods of time, you also had your birth; you were born of a virgin, of one that had no knowledge of any man. To redeem us from the Law, you submitted to the

Law. Your purpose was to free us from the slavery to which our corruption had reduced us and to confer upon us the rank of sons.

This is the day when you were carried to the temple and the aged Simeon took you in his arms and asked leave to go in peace. "My own eyes have seen," he said, "your grace and your saving power."

Deliver us, now, Lord, from all that is vain; fulfill your promise and free us from sin and shame; fill our hearts with your Holy Spirit and enable us to say: "Abba, Father."

Make us true sons of your Father. Protect us against all the evil in the world. Grant that we may celebrate this feast in peace. Accept your servants' petitions, as you accepted the confession of Anna, the prophetess. Instead of a pair of turtledoves or two young pigeons, take the pure homage of the worship we offer you. And fill us with the good things that are in your kingdom. All this we ask with your Mother and holy old Simeon, with Anna the prophetess and all the other saints.

PRESENTATION FROM A SYRIAC LITURGY

THE radiance of the Father's splendor, the Father's visible image, Jesus Christ our God, peerless among counselors, Prince of peace, Father of the world to come, the model after which Adam was formed, for our sakes became like a slave: in the womb of Mary the Virgin, without assistance from any man, he took flesh. For our sakes he was wrapped in swaddling clothes, laid in a manger, and praised by the angelic powers.

"Glory to God in high heaven," they sang; "peace and good will to men."

Enable us, Lord, to reach the end of this luminous feast

in peace, forsaking all idle words, acting virtuously, shunning our passions, and raising ourselves above the things of this world.

Bless your Church, which you brought into being long ago and attached to yourself through your own life-giving blood. Help all orthodox pastors, heads of churches, and doctors.

Bless your servants, whose trust is all in you; bless all Christian souls, the sick, those tormented by evil spirits, and those who have asked us to pray for them.

Show yourself as merciful as you are rich in grace; save and preserve us; enable us to obtain those good things to come which will never know an end.

May we celebrate your glorious birth, and the Father who sent you to redeem us, and your Spirit, the Giver of life, now and forever, age after age. Amen.

PRAYER FROM A SYRIAC CHRISTMAS LITURGY

BE off, Satan, from this door and from these four walls. This is no place for you; there is nothing for you to do here. This is the place for Peter and Paul and the holy Gospel; and this is where I mean to sleep, now that my worship is done, in the name of the Father and of the Holy Spirit.

In the name of our Lord Jesus Christ, send me your Spirit; instill the wisdom of your Holy Spirit into my heart; protect my soul and body, every limb in my body, every fiber of my being, from all possible harm and all traps the Devil may set for me and every temptation to sin. Teach me to give you thanks, O Father, Son, and Holy Spirit.

EUCHOLOGIUM SINAITICUM

III. Post-Nicene Prayers

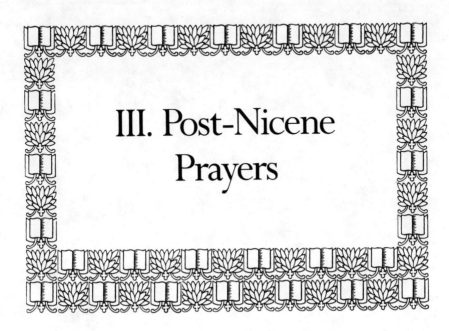

WITH the conversion of the Emperor Constantine to Christianity, at long last the period of persecution was over and the Church flourished. So did Christian theology, though peace here did not reign. A new war of words between various theological schools was waged with nearly as much passion as was devoted before to their common attacks on Roman state religion, pagan mystery cults, and Gnostic sectarians. Here the battles were fought in theological tracts and won (or lost) at great councils, where the leaders of the Church hammered out creedal language that persists to this very day. But when the great theologians spoke directly to God, their prayerful devotions transcended allegiance to party. Though distinctive theological elements can be discerned when contrasting fourth- and fifth-century prayers written in Rome, Constantinople, Antioch, Egypt, and elsewhere, when viewed from a remove of a millennium and a half, these distinctions pale when compared to the common faith these beautiful prayers express.

Perhaps more evident are differences in literary style and devotional language. The Greek prayers in Chapter Seven are distinguished by literary sophistication and elegance. Saint Gregory Nazianzus in particular was one of the great poets of the early Church. Long before converting to Christianity, Basil the Great, Basil's brother, Gregory of Nyssa, and sister, Macrina the Younger, studied the Greek poets and philosophers in school, and their talent for expression was cultivated accordingly. And Saint John Chrysostom, the golden-tongued orator, adapted the Greek rhetorical traditions to masterful effect.

Many of the Syriac prayers collected in Chapter Eight are shaped in part by the same tradition but are distinctive in their lavishness and formal spontaneity. This is especially evident in the fifth-century prayers of Balai and Rabbula. Their fourth-century predecessor, Ephraem the Syrian, was known as the "Lyre of the Holy Spirit." Several of these prayers witness to ongoing persecution in the Eastern church. The Coptic prayers contained in the same chapter express a more mystical and ascetic approach to the deity. Both Macarius and Shenute lived most of their lives in the desert as monks.

The Latin prayers of Chapter Nine comprise a representative sample of Western devotional literature of the fourth and fifth centuries. In general more formally austere and conventionally structured than the Eastern prayers, these prayers also show the influence of Eastern devotional traditions. In particular, Saint Ambrose draws much of his inspiration from Origen, and in turn will himself have a profound influence on Saint Augustine. The four Irish prayers from Saints Patrick and Brigid of Gael, colorful and filled with music, stand in a category of their own.

SEVEN

Prayers from Greek Sources

MAY the very God of all things, who spoke by the Holy Spirit, through the prophets, and sent him forth upon the apostles here in Jerusalem on the day of Pentecost, send him forth now upon you also, and through him guard us, imparting his bounty in common to all of us, so as to exhibit always the fruits of the Holy Spirit, charity, joy, peace, patience, benignity, goodness, faith, mildness, chastity, in Christ Jesus our Lord, through whom, and with whom, together with the Holy Spirit, be glory to the Father, now and always and for ever and ever. Amen.

SAINT CYRIL OF JERUSALEM

LORD our God, teach us, we beseech thee, to ask thee aright for the right blessings. Steer thou the vessel of our life toward thyself, thou tranquil Haven of all storm-tossed souls. Show us the course wherein we should go. Renew a willing spirit within us. Let thy Spirit curb our wayward senses, and guide and enable us unto that which is our true good, to keep thy laws, and in all our works evermore to rejoice in thy glorious and gladdening Presence. For thine is the glory and praise from all thy saints for ever and ever. Amen.

SAINT BASIL

FOR thou verily, O Lord, art the pure and eternal Fount of goodness, who didst justly turn away from us, and in loving kindness didst have mercy upon us. Thou didst hate, and wert reconciled; thou didst curse, and didst bless; thou didst banish us from Paradise, and didst recall us; thou didst strip off the fig tree leaves, an unseemly covering, and put upon us a costly garment; thou didst open the prison, and didst release the condemned; thou didst sprinkle us with clean water, and cleanse us from our filthiness. No longer shall Adam be confounded when called by thee, nor hide himself, convicted by his conscience, cowering in the thicket of Paradise. Nor shall the flaming sword encircle Paradise around, and make the entrance inaccessible to those who draw near; but all is turned to joy for us that were the heirs of sin: Paradise, yea, Heaven itself may be trodden by man: and the creation, in the world and above the world, that once was at variance with itself, is knit together in friendship: and we men are made to join in the angels' song, offering the worship of their praise to God. For all these things then let us sing to God that hymn of joy, which lips touched by the Spirit long ago sang loudly: "Let my soul be joyful in the Lord: for he hath clothed me with a garment of salvation, and hath put upon me a robe of gladness: as on a bridegroom he hath set a miter upon me, and as a bride hath he adorned me with fair array." And verily the Adorner of the bride is Christ, who is, and was, and shall be, blessed now and for evermore. Amen.

SAINT GREGORY OF NYSSA

LORD, you have taken the fear of death away from us. The end of our life here you have made the beginning of the true life. For a little while you will let our bodies rest in sleep, and then with the last trumpet you will wake them from their sleep.

You give to the earth to keep for you this earth of ours, which you shaped with your own hands; and you will take it back again, and from a mortal, formless lump transform it into a thing of immortal beauty.

To free us from sin and from the curse laid upon us, you took both sin and the curse upon yourself.

You crushed the head of the dragon that had seized men by the throat and thrust them into the gulf prepared for the disobedient.

When you shattered the gates of Hell and trampled the Devil, death's lord, beneath your feet, you cleared the way for our resurrection.

To us who fear you you gave a sign, the sign of your holy cross, to destroy the Enemy and infuse new vigor into our lives.

O eternal God, you have been my refuge ever since I left my mother's womb; I love you with all my inmost strength; I have devoted myself body and soul to you from childhood onwards.

Set now an angel of light beside me and bid him take my hand and lead me to the resting place where there is water for refreshment, beside the dwellings of the holy fathers.

The flaming sword you snapped in two; the man who hung upon the cross with you and implored your great mercy you restored to Paradise. Remember me, too, now that you are back in your kingdom, since I also have hung upon the cross with you and the nails have pierced my flesh; for I have always feared you and feared your judgment. May the dread gulf not divide me from your elect or the slanderer stand in my way; may your eyes not rest on my sins.

If out of the weakness of human nature I have fallen and sinned in word or deed or thought, forgive it me; for you have power to forgive sins on earth. When I am divested of my body, may I stand before you with my soul unspotted: receive it, blameless and faultless, with your own hands.

SAINT MACRINA

O Christ my King. You turned aside the dire might of Amelech, when your servant Moses raised his pure hands after the pattern of the cross in prayer upon the mountain. You fettered the savage jaws of lions and the sharp strength of their claws for Daniel's sake when he stretched out his hands. When Jonah opened wide his arms in prayer within the monster's entrails, he was delivered by your power from the whale. And when the three young men in the Assyrian furnace boldly raised their arms, you spread about them a moist cloud. Once, in order to deliver the storm-tossed disciples from the waters, you trod on foot the face of the turbulent deep stilling the waves' and the winds' might. For many a person you have rescued soul and body from disease. You who are God became man and mingled with mortals.

God from all time, you were manifested to us in the fullness of time, so that by becoming man you might make me God. Thus, when I call on you, come as blessed and propitious God. Come to me with helping hand, O my propitious God. Save me, overwhelmed as I am amid war, and wild beasts, and fire, and storm. I have nowhere to turn my gaze except to God alone. All this is brought upon me by evil men, the destroyers of life—wild beasts, the fierce swell of the sea, the horrors of war, the onset of fierce fire. Their chief animosity is directed against people who love God. They do not stand in awe of the coming judgment, and they make of no account the man who hates evil.

From these, O Christ, deliver me. Spread your sheltering wings about me always. O King, drive hateful cares far from your servant. Let not my mind be harassed by grave anxieties, such as this world and the prince of this world devise for hapless mortals. They corrode the godlike image within as rust corrodes iron. The nobler form they reduce to kinship with the earth, so that the soul cannot succeed in elevating the earthbound element of flesh. On the contrary, the flesh drags the winged soul earthwards in misery, enfleshing it in sordid activities.

SAINT GREGORY NAZIANZUS

CHRIST, give me strength: your servant is not what he
was.
The tongue that praised you idle? How can you bear it?
Give your priest strength, do not cast him off.
O to be well again, to preach once more
salvation and to wash the people clean.
Do not forsake me, my Strength, I beseech you.
When the storm beat hard I may have betrayed you,
but let me return to you now.

SAINT GREGORY NAZIANZUS

SAVE me, save me, Immortal,
from the Enemy's hand;
let no evil-doing defeat me
or Pharaoh torment me;
let me not be his captive,
Christ, your Opponent's;
let him not wound me and drag me
to hardhearted Babylon.

I would live forever in your temple,
singing your praises,
safe from the showers of Sodom,
from the flames on the head,
all evil dispelled by the shadow
of your powerful hand.

SAINT GREGORY NAZIANZUS

ALAS, I neither care to live nor die,
for life means sin and after death comes judgment.
Trembling I stand between them; flames flow round me.
Courage from Christ I take: no power of mine
is equal to the struggle with existence.
If to remain a while upon this earth
will cleanse me from my sins, it will be well;
but if my woes increase, then, while there's time,
O let me die, lest worse should overtake me.

SAINT GREGORY NAZIANZUS

I rise and pledge myself to God
to do no deed at all of dark.
This day shall be his sacrifice
and I, unmoved, my passions' lord.
I blush to be so old and foul
and yet to stand before his table.
You know what I would do, O Christ;
O then, to do it make me able.

SAINT GREGORY NAZIANZUS

I am spent, O my Christ, Breath of my life.
Perpetual stress and surge, in league together,
make long, O long, this life, this business of living.
Grappling with foes within and foes without,
my soul hast lost its beauty, blurred your image.

Did ever oak such buffeting from winds
or ship receive from waves as I do now?
Labor to labor, task succeeds to task.
Even my Father's house, received in trust
reluctantly, I've found in dust and ruins.

Friendship has bowed and illness wasted me.
Stones for my welcome, not a flower I've had.
The folk the Spirit gave to me is gone:
this child I've had to leave, this left me, that
cares naught for me. Heavy the father's heart.

My fellow priests are more than enemies;
the mystic table draws no reverence
from them; they scorn these sufferings of mine
that sometimes from the worst have won respect.
One only thing they long for: my disgrace.

SAINT GREGORY NAZIANZUS

I have deceived myself, dear Christ, I confess it;
I have fallen from the heights to the depths.
O lift me up again, for well I know
delusion came because I wanted it.
If I presume again, I'll fall again,
and fall to my undoing. Take me to you
or I die. It cannot be that I
alone shall find you hard and unresponsive.

SAINT GREGORY NAZIANZUS

ALAS, dear Christ, the Dragon is here again.
Alas, he is here: terror has seized me, and fear.
Alas that I ate of the fruit of the tree of knowledge.
Alas that his envy led me to envy too.
I did not become like God; I was cast out of Paradise.
Temper, sword, awhile, the heat of your flames
and let me go again about the garden,
entering with Christ, a thief from another tree.

SAINT GREGORY NAZIANZUS

LIFE is a burden; most of it gone,
I would be gone with it too,
for evil, alas, will not be bowed down.
Breath of all mortals, lengthen my days
or out of the reach of misfortune
set me and stablish me; that would be kindness.
If you will not, I must die.

SAINT GREGORY NAZIANZUS

O Lord God Almighty, who knowest the thoughts of men, who searchest the hearts, the reins, and who, to this thy holy mystery hast called me, as I am, unworthy: Do thou loathe not me, neither turn thou thy face from me away, but wipe away all my transgressions; wash away the filth of my body, wash away the defilements of my soul and thoroughly sanctify me, so that while praying thy goodness to grant forgiveness of sins to others, I myself be not cast away. O Lord: Do not turn me away, lowly as I am, ashamed! Send upon me the grace of the Holy Ghost: make me worthy before thy holy altar thus to stand!

SAINT GREGORY NAZIANZUS

LABOR awaits you, soul, great labor,
if you would know yourself,
the what, the whither, and the whence,
the way of now behaving—
whether it should be as it is
or whether more is expected;
labor awaits you, soul, and a purer life.

If you would ponder on God and probe
into his mysteries,
if you would know what was there before
the world and the world itself—
the source from which it came to you,
the end that will take it from you:
labor awaits you, soul, and a purer life.

If you would know how God guides the helm
of the world and the course he plots,
why he set some things like rocks in the sea

while others he left in flux—
why men most of all are caught in the stream
and the swirl of perpetual change:
labor awaits you, soul, and a purer life.

If you would show me my former glory,
the shame that has come to succeed it,
what binds me to this mortal life
and what my end will be—
if you would hold this light to my mind
and drive dark error from it:
labor awaits you, soul; may it not undo you.

SAINT GREGORY NAZIANZUS

GREAT you are, Pasch (I mean to speak to you, you see, as if you were a living person); holy you are, cleansing the world from all its stains.

Word spoken by God, light, life, wisdom, power: all these names are yours, and I use them all to greet you with. Fruit, invention, image of the great Mind; as word spiritual, as human visible; firmly uttered by God to be the support of all things and to bind them together: accept this address, even though it is not the beginning of my career, but its end. Take it as a thanksgiving, take it as a prayer that I may have nothing to suffer beyond those necessary trials, those holy trials which I have known all my life long. Check the power my body has over me—you know, Lord, what it is like, how burdensome it is; and do not be in a hurry to condemn me when it comes to my purification. May my prayers be answered; may I find a welcome in Heaven. Here and now I will offer on your holy altar a sacrifice you will be glad to receive, O Father, Word, and Holy Spirit.

Glory, honor, and power are your due, in all their various forms, throughout the endless succession of ages. Amen.

SAINT GREGORY NAZIANZUS

O Lord and maker of all, and especially of this body of ours! O God and Father and pilot of thine own mankind! O master of life and death! O guardian and benefactor of our souls! O thou who makest and changest all seasonably by thy creative word, even as thou knowest in the depth of thy wisdom and providence, receive Caesarius now, the first fruits of our pilgrimage! And if the last is first, we yield to thy word, by which the universe is ruled. And receive us also afterwards in due time, having directed us in the flesh as long as it is for our advantage. And receive us, ready and not troubled by fear of thee, nor turning away in our last days, nor forcibly drawn from things of earth, as is the misfortune of souls loving the world and the flesh, but eagerly drawn to the heavenly life, everlasting and blessed, which is in Christ Jesus our Lord, to whom be glory for ever and ever. Amen.

SAINT GREGORY NAZIANZUS

COME away from Lebanon, bride, for you are fair in every part and there is no fault to be found in you.

Paradise of the great Architect, city of the holy King, bride of the spotless Christ, pure in virginity, faithfully promised in marriage to the one Husband, radiant and shining like the dawn: Fair you are as the moon, majestic as the sun, inspiring awe as an army does drawn up for battle.

Queens call you blessed, concubines sing your praises, maidservants proclaim their respect for you.

Dazzling the sight of you as you come up from the desert, . . . scented vapors enclosing you.

Like a column of smoke you come up from the desert, breathing out myrrh and incense, sweeter than all the scents the perfumer has given his powders. Well did he know it who foretold of you: "Your very name soothes the heart like flow of myrrh; what wonder the maids should love you?"

Your place is at the King's right hand, your robe is of gold, fringed and embroidered. . . .

With you there is safety from heresy's hateful designs and shelter from the storms it raises; with you, holy mother Church, we take heart again, with you and with your holy teaching, which alone tells us what we may truly believe about God.

EPIPHANIUS OF SALAMIS

SO let us be sober and watchful, and prepared for everything, so that we may be well disciplined in prosperity and restrained under the onset of adversity, showing great prudence and constantly rendering thanks to the loving God. . . . and thus be able to pass our life on earth securely and have much confidence regarding the life to come. May we all reach it, through the love and goodness of our Lord Jesus Christ, to whom, with the Father and the Holy Spirit, be glory, sovereignty, and praise, now and forever, for ages of ages. Amen.

SAINT JOHN CHRYSOSTOM

EIGHT

Prayers from Syriac and Coptic Sources

YOU are rich in grace and mercy, you are willing to cleanse all sinners from their guilt. Cleanse me with hyssop, have pity on me. In your mercy spare me, as you spared the publican and the sinful woman. You take the sinfulness from sinners, O Christ, and when we repent you make us welcome beside you. Redeemer of the human race, in your mercy save me.

If salvation is hard for even the just to obtain, what will become of me, sinner that I am? I have not borne the day's burden or the sun's heat; I am one of those workmen who came at the eleventh hour. Save me, have pity on me.

My sins have bowed me to the ground and cast me down from the heights where I sat enthroned. I could not have been more determined on my own ruin if I had rushed over a precipice. Who but you can restore to me the beauty I had at first, O wisest of Creators—who but you, who made me in the first place like yourself, made me an image of yourself? It was my own free choice that made me an accomplice of the Devil and a slave of sin. Deliver me, Lord, in your mercy; have pity on me.

My thoughts confuse me and cloud my mind; I am in despair because my guilt is vaster than the ocean and my sins outnumber the waves in the sea. Yet I have heard your gracious words: "Call and I shall hear you; knock and I will open the door for you." I call, then, to you like the sinful woman in the Gospel, I entreat you like the publican and the prodigal son. I have sinned against Heaven and before you.

Deliver my soul from its sin, O Saviour, as you delivered theirs, for my misdeeds have kindled your wrath. In your mercy have pity on me.

When I remember how I have fallen, I tremble at the thought of your justice, for you are well aware of my sores and stains. I dare not look upwards, because my sins reach as high as the heavens; the mere sight of the earth is an accusation to me, for my offenses exceed the number of its inhabitants.

Sorry my plight will be when the just and the saints come before God, their good deeds shining like the sun. What will become of me, Lord, and my lusterless works?

Sorry my plight will be when the priests come forward and give you back the talents they received from you. I buried mine, Lord, in the ground. What shall I find to say? What answer shall I be able to make?

I am determined that the fire shall not consume me, since you have given me your body and blood to feed me. I refuse to be carried off to Hell, for you have given me baptism as a garment to clothe me.

Grant me the dew of your grace, and in your mercy, Lord, forgive me my sins; but above all, may glory be yours.

RABBULA OF EDESSA

GIVE me this crown, Lord; you know how I long for it, for I have loved you with all my heart and all my being. When I see you, I shall be filled with joy and you will give me rest. I shall no longer have to live in this world and see my people suffering, your churches destroyed, your altars overthrown, your devoted clergy everywhere persecuted, the weak defiled, the lukewarm turned from the truth, and my flock that was so large reduced at the time of testing to a handful.

I shall not see the many that seemed to be my friends undergo an inward change, become hostile and seek my death; or find those that were my friends for a while taken from me by persecution, at the very time when the killers are snapping their fingers at our people and lording it over them.

Yet I mean to persevere in my vocation like a hero and to walk bravely along the path marked out for me, so that I shall be an example to all your people in the East. I have had the first place at table, I will have the first place too when it comes to dying; I will be the first to give my blood. Then with my brethren I shall enter on that life in which there are no cares, no anxiety, no solicitude, a life where there is neither persecutor nor persecuted, neither oppressor nor oppressed, neither tyrant nor victim of tyranny. No threatening kings, no blustering prefects shall I see there. No one there will cite me before his tribunal or upset me with repeated menaces; there will be no one to do me violence or bully me.

I shall stumble no more, when once I have gained a firm footing in you, the Way we all must walk in. My weary limbs will find their rest in you, for you, Anointed, are the Oil that is to anoint us. The grief in my heart will be forgotten when I drink of you, the Chalice of our salvation. The tears in my eyes you will wipe away, O Joy, O Consolation.

SIMEON OF PERSIA

MY God: without ceasing, I will tread the threshold of thy house. I will ask with boldness, that I may receive with confidence.

For if, O Lord, the earth enriches manifold a single grain of wheat, how then shall my prayers be enriched by thy grace!

Because of the voices of my children, their sighs and their groans, open to me the door of thy mercy: make glad their voices, the mourning of their sackcloth.

For a flock, O my Lord, in the field, if so be it has seen the wolves, flees to the shepherd, and takes refuge under his staff, and he drives them that would devour it.

Thy flock has seen the wolves, and lo! it cries loudly. Behold: how terrified it is! Let thy cross be a staff, to drive them that would swallow it up!

Accept the cry of my little ones, that are altogether pure. It was he, the Infant of days, that could appease, O Lord, the Ancient of days.

The day when the Babe came down, in the midst of the staff, the watchers descended and proclaimed peace: may that peace be, in all my streets, for all my offspring.

Have mercy, O Lord, on my children! In my children, call to mind thy childhood, thou who wast a child! Let them that are like thy childhood be saved by thy grace!

SAINT EPHRAEM THE SYRIAN

O God born of God, true God of the true God born, you are goodness itself, we confess it. In your kindness come to our aid. May we never know the day when we shall have to share with Satan the pains of Hell. Be merciful and hide us under the shadow of your wings.

We acknowledge that you are the Light. We are as

servants in your hands; do not allow the Evil One to snatch us from you; prevent us from rebelling against your sovereignty.

We know that you are just: show us your justice, Lord. We know that you are our Saviour: deliver us, save us from evil. We acknowledge your holiness: make us holy through your body and blood. Having eaten your flesh and drunk your precious blood, may the elect sing your praises.

Grant us forgiveness, kind God, merciful as you are to sinners.

SAINT EPHRAEM THE SYRIAN

O Lord Jesus Christ, King of kings: you have power over life and death, you know even what is uncertain and obscure, our thoughts and feelings are no secret from you. Cleanse me from my hidden faults, for I have done evil and you have seen it.

Day by day my life draws nearer to its end and my sins increase in number. O Lord, God of spirits and of all corporeal creatures, you know how frail I am, in soul and in body. Give me strength, Lord, in my weakness and uphold me in my sufferings.

Knowing that I have come to be regarded by many people as an oddity, you strengthen and support me. Give me a prudent judgment, good Lord, and let me always remember your blessings. Do not think of my many sins; put my faults out of your mind.

Lord, do not disdain my prayer, a sinner's though it is and worthless; but leave with me until the end that grace of yours that has been my protection until now. Your grace it was that taught me wisdom. Blessed are they that keep to its paths; a glorious crown awaits them.

I am unworthy and sinful, Lord, but still I bless and praise you, for you have poured your mercies lavishly over me; you have been my Helper and Protector; your great name deserves eternal glory.

Glory to you, O Lord, our God.

SAINT EPHRAEM THE SYRIAN

O Lord God, Ruler of the heaven and of the earth, Creator of things visible and invisible, Giver of eternal life, and Consoler of the sorrowful, make me to stand firm in the confession of thy name that as with thine aid I have begun the good fight, so with thine aid I may be deemed worthy to gain the victory, lest the adversary spitefully mock at me, saying: "Where is now her God in whom she trusted?"

But let the angel of thy light come and restore to me the light which the darkness of my cell has taken from me; and let the right hand of thy majesty scatter the phantom hosts of the ancient enemy. For we know, O Lord, that thy mercy will aid us in all temptations.

MARGARET OF ANTIOCH

IT needs no more than three to meet in your name for a Church to come into being. There are thousands assembled here: give them your protection. Their hearts had built this sanctuary to the glory of your name before ever hand laid one stone on another. May the temples we build within ourselves be as beautiful as the temple built of stone. May your kindness impel you to live in both kinds of temple, for our hearts, no less than these stones, bear the mark of your name.

God, who is all-powerful, could have made himself a house as easily as he brought the world into existence, with a wave of his hand. But he preferred to build man instead, and man in turn was to build for him. Blessed be the mercy that showed us such love.

He is infinite and we are finite; he built us the world and we build him a house. What a wonderful thing it is that men can build a house for the God of all power, who is present everywhere, whom nothing escapes.

He lives among us, such is his affection for us; he binds us to himself with his love. He has come to stay with us and he urges us to take the road to Heaven, to go and live with him.

If he left his dwelling and chose to live in the Church, it was to persuade us to abandon our homes and choose Paradise instead. God came to live among men that men might come into contact with God.

Yours is the kingdom of Heaven, the house of God is ours; and building the house, the workmen merit the kingdom. There the priest offers bread in your name and you give your flock your body to eat.

Where are you, Lord? In Heaven.

Where shall we expect to find you? Here in the sanctuary.

Your heavens are too high for us, but the Church is within our reach and we can find you there.

Your throne in Heaven rests on a bank of flame: who would dare to approach it? But the God of all power lives also in bread: whoever will may approach and taste.

BALAI

IT was at the end of time that you came, O God, to save us; the light was failing when you drove Adam from Paradise and when you opened the gates to let him in again. Remember your death on the cross and be merciful, now that the end of my life is approaching, now that the evening awaits me. Time is too short for me to wash all my sins away. There are so many of them. I cannot ask for as many years in which to make amends.

Spare me, Lord, when I appear before your terrible tribunal; have pity on me, God, for there will be limits then to your mercy. Cast me a look as you give your verdicts in all their severity, and let me see the peace and gentleness in your face.

Heal me while I am still on earth and I shall have health indeed. In your mercy raise me up and bring me to repentance, so that when I meet you in Heaven I shall have no cause for shame. Do not leave me, Lord, in my enemies' power; do not let me fall a prey to those who set snares for my soul; do not let me lose your grace or the gift of the Spirit.

Lord, I will wash the stains from my garment, for I do not want to be cast into the darkness without, like the man who was judged unfit to be at the feast. Enable me to keep my lamp full of oil, as your servants must if they are to win your approval, and then I shall not be refused admittance like the foolish virgins. Spare me, Lord, those terrifying words that you keep for those on your left; do not say to me: "I do not know you."

Through the blood which you shed on the cross for me, give me life, for you are merciful. May I always bear witness to your word and live for your glory; may delight be mine in your kingdom forever. Amen.

MACARIUS OF EGYPT

HOLY angel, to whose care this poor soul and wretched body of mine have been given, do not cast me off because I am a sinner, do not hold aloof from me because I am not clean. Do not yield your place to the Spirit of Evil; guide me by your influence on my mortal body.

Take my limp hand and bring me to the path that leads to salvation.

Yes, holy angel, God has given you charge of my miserable little soul and body. Forgive every deed of mine that has ever offended you at any time in my life; forgive the sins I have committed today. Protect me during the coming night and keep me safe from the machinations and contrivances of the Enemy, that I may not sin and arouse God's anger.

Intercede for me with the Lord; ask him to make me fear him more and more, and to enable me to give him the service his goodness deserves. Amen.

MACARIUS OF EGYPT

O God, watch over me always, in my work, in my words, in the thoughts of my heart.

O God, have pity on me, in this world and in the world to come.

O God, have pity on me, for I have sinned against you like the mortal that I am; but, kind and gentle Master, forgive me.

O God, may I not be afraid or disturbed when the time comes for my soul to leave my body.

O God, do not be angry then and rebuke me, do not give vent to wrath and punish me.

O God, do not show me the anger that my sins and misdeeds deserve.

O God, do not hide your face from me when I come before you, do not turn away from me when you pronounce your sentence on our lives—the lives we have lived openly and the lives that have been ours in secret.

O God, your Word was made flesh for me; for me he was crucified, died, was buried, and on the third day rose again. Bind me to you, and let no evil spirit lord it over me and snatch me out of your hands.

O God, do not let me give way to disloyalty. May the Enemy find nothing in me that he can call his own.

O God, sharpen my will. May it be like a sword and cut all sinful thoughts out of my mind.

O God, as you calmed the sea with a word, so drive out the evil passions from my sinful nature. May sin die down and disappear from all my members.

O God, grant that my heart may always be pure and my faith orthodox forever, yes forever. Amen.

SHENUTE

NINE

Prayers from Latin Sources

O Lord:
Keep us from vain strife or words:
Grant to us a constant
Profession of the truth!
Preserve us in the faith,
True faith and undefiled,
That ever we may hold fast
That which we professed when we were baptized
Unto, and in the name of,
Father,
The Son,
The Holy Ghost—
That we may have thee
For our Father,
That in thy Son
We may abide,
And in the fellowship of the Holy Ghost:
Through the same Jesus Christ,
Our Lord. Amen.

SAINT HILARY OF POITIERS

SO long as I shall have the power by means of this spirit whom thou hast granted me, Holy Father, almighty God, I will confess thee to be not only eternally God, but also eternally Father. Nor will I ever break out into such folly and impiety, as to make myself the judge of thy omnipotence and thy mysteries, nor shall this weak understanding arrogantly seek for more than that devout belief in thy infinitude and faith in thy eternity, which have been taught me. I will not assert that thou wast ever without thy wisdom, and thy power, and thy Word, without God only-begotten, my Lord Jesus Christ. The weak and imperfect language, to which our nature is limited, does not dominate my thoughts concerning thee, so that my poverty of utterance should choke faith into silence. For although we have a word and wisdom and power of our own, the product of our free inward activity, yet thine is the absolute generation of perfect God, who is thy Word and Wisdom and Power; so that he can never be separated from thee, who in these names of thy eternal properties is shewn to be born of thee. Yet his birth is only so far shewn as to make manifest the fact that thou art the source of his being; yet sufficiently to confirm our belief in his infinity, inasmuch as it is related that he was born before times eternal.

For in human affairs thou hast set before us many things of such a sort, that though we do not know their cause, yet the effect is not unknown; and reverence inculcates faith, where ignorance is inherent in our nature. Thus when I raised to thy Heaven these feeble eyes of mine, my certainty regarding it was limited to the fact that it is thine. For seeing therein these orbits where the stars are fixed, and their annual revolutions, and the Pleiades and the Great Bear and the Morning Star, each having their varied duties in the service which is appointed them, I recognize thy presence, O God, in these things whereof I cannot gain any clear understanding. And when I view the marvelous swellings of thy sea, I know that I have failed to comprehend not merely the origin of the waters but even the movements of this changeful expanse; yet I grasp at faith in some reasonable cause, although it is one that I cannot see, and fail not to recognize thee in these things also, which I do not know. Furthermore, when in thought I turn to the earth, which by the power of hidden agencies causes to decay all the seeds which it receives, quickens them when decayed, multiplies them when quickened, and makes them strong when multiplied; in all these changes I find nothing which my mind can understand, yet my ignorance helps toward recognizing thee, for though I know nothing of the nature that waits on me, I recognize thee by actual experience of the advantages I possess. Moreover, though I do not know myself, yet I perceive so much that I marvel at thee the more because I am ignorant of myself. For without understanding it, I perceive a certain motion or order or life in my mind when it exercises its powers; and this very perception I owe to thee, for though thou deniest the power of understanding my natural first beginning, yet thou givest that of perceiving nature with its charms. And since in what concerns myself I recognize thee, ignorant as I am, so recognizing thee I will not in what concerns thee cherish a feebler faith in thy omnipotence, because I do not understand. My thoughts shall not attempt to grasp and master the origin of thy only-begotten Son, nor shall my faculties strain to reach beyond the truth that he is my Creator and my God.

SAINT HILARY OF POITIERS

AND now, almighty God, I first must pray thee to forgive my excess of indignation, and permit me to address thee; and next to grant me, dust and ashes as I am, yet bound in loyal devotion to thyself, freedom of utterance in this debate. There was a time when I, poor wretch, was not; before my life and consciousness and personality began to exist. It is to thy mercy that I owe my life; and I doubt not that thou, in thy goodness, didst give me my birth for my good, for thou, who hast no need of me, wouldst never have made the beginning of my life the beginning of evil. And then, when thou hadst breathed into me the breath of life and endowed me with the power of thought, thou didst instruct me in the knowledge of thyself, by means of the sacred volumes given us through thy servants, Moses and the prophets. From them I learnt thy revelation, that we must not worship thee as a lonely God. For their pages taught me of God, not different from thee in nature but one with thee in mysterious unity of substance. I learnt that thou art God in God, by no mingling or confusion but by thy very nature, since the divinity which is thyself dwells in him who is from thee. But the true doctrine of the perfect birth revealed that thou, the Indwelt, and thou, the Indweller, are not One Person, yet that thou dost dwell in him who is from thee. And the voices of evangelists and apostles repeat the lesson, and the very words which fell from the holy mouth of thy only-begotten are recorded, telling how thy Son, God the only-begotten from thee the unbegotten God, was born of the Virgin as man to fulfill the mystery of my salvation; how thou dwellest in him, by virtue of his true generation from thyself, and he in thee, because of the nature given in his abiding birth from thee.

What is this hopeless quagmire of error into which thou hast plunged me? For I have learnt all this and have come to believe it; this faith is so ingrained into my mind that I have neither the power nor the wish to change it. Why this deception of an unhappy man, this ruin of a poor wretch in body and soul, by deluding him with falsehoods concerning thyself? After the Red Sea had been divided, the splendor on the face of Moses, descending from the Mount, deceived me. He had gazed, in thy presence, upon all the mysteries of Heaven, and I believed his words, dictated by thee, concerning thyself. And David, the man that was found after thine own heart, has betrayed me to destruction, and Solomon, who was thought worthy of the gift of divine wisdom, and Isaiah, who saw the Lord of Sabaoth and prophesied, and Jeremiah consecrated in the womb before he was fashioned, to be the prophet of nations to be rooted out and planted in, and Ezekiel, the witness of the mystery of the resurrection, and Daniel, the man beloved, who had knowledge of times, and all the hallowed band of the prophets; and Matthew also, chosen to proclaim the whole mystery of the Gospel, first a publican, then an apostle, and John, the Lord's familiar friend, and therefore worthy to reveal the deepest secrets of Heaven, and blessed Simon, who after his confession of the mystery was set to be the foundation stone of the Church, and received the keys of the kingdom of Heaven, and all his companions who spoke by the Holy Ghost, and Paul, the chosen vessel, changed from persecutor into apostle, who, as a living man, abode under the deep sea and ascended into the third Heaven, who was in Paradise before his martyrdom, whose martyrdom was the perfect offering of a flawless faith; all have deceived me.

These are the men who have taught me the doctrines which I hold, and so deeply am I impregnated with their teaching that no antidote can release me from their influence. Forgive me, O God Almighty, my powerlessness to change, my willingness to die in this belief. These propagators of blasphemy, for so they seem to me, are a product of these last times, too modern to avail me. It is too late for them to correct the faith which I received from thee. Before I had ever heard their names, I had put my trust in thee, had received regeneration from thee and become thine, as still I am. I know that thou art omnipotent; I look not that thou shouldst reveal to me the mystery of that ineffable birth which is secret between thyself and thy only-begotten. Nothing is impossible with thee, and I doubt not that in begetting thy Son thou didst exert thy full omnipotence. To doubt it would be to deny that thou art omnipotent. For my own birth teaches me that thou art good, and therefore I am sure that in the birth of thine Only-begotten thou didst grudge him no good gift. I believe that all that is thine is his, and all that is his is thine. The creation of the world is sufficient evidence to me that thou art wise; and I am sure that thy Wisdom, who is like thee, must have been begotten from thyself. And thou art one God, in very truth, in my eyes; I will never believe that in him, who is God from thee, there is aught that is not thine. Judge me in him, if it be sin in me that, through thy Son, I have trusted too well in Law and prophets and apostles.

SAINT HILARY OF POITIERS

O gracious Lord, Jesus Christ! I, a sinner, presuming nothing on my merits, trusting in thy mercy and thy goodness, with fear and in trembling approach the table of thy most sweet feast, for my heart, my body, are stained with many sins, my thoughts and lips not diligently guarded. Wherefore, O gracious God, O awful Majesty, in my extremity I turn to thee, the Fount of Mercy. To thee I hasten to be healed, to take refuge under thy protection, and thee, before whom as my judge I cannot stand, I long for as my Saviour.

To thee, O Lord, I show my wounds. I know my many and great sins for which I am afraid. My trust is in thy mercies, of which there is no end. Look, therefore, on me with eyes of thy mercy, O Lord, Jesus Christ, God and Man. Hearken unto me, whose trust is in thee: upon me, mercy!—who am full of misery and sin.

O thou! Fount of Mercy that will never cease to flow—hail! saving Victim! Hail! noble and precious Blood, flowing from the wounds of my crucified Lord and Saviour, Jesus Christ! Wash away my sins! Be mindful, O Lord, of thy creature, whom thou hast redeemed with thine own blood. I repent that I have sinned. I desire to amend what I have done. Take, therefore, from me, O most merciful Father, all my iniquities away, and all my sins, that, being cleansed both in body and in soul, I worthily may taste thy Holy of Holies. Grant that this holy feeding on thy body, on thy blood, of which I propose to partake, unworthy as I am, may be for the remission of my sins, and may be perfect cleansing of my soul, the driving away of all evil spirits, the renewal of all holy desires, the bringing forth fully of the fruit well pleasing to thee, and the most sure protection of my soul, my body, against the wiles of all my enemies, and thine. Amen.

SAINT AMBROSE

O God Almighty, who didst cleanse the lips of the prophet Isaiah with a burning coal: Cleanse my heart and my lips: so vouchsafe to cleanse me, of thy mercy, that I may be able to proclaim worthily thy holy Gospel: through Jesus Christ our Lord. Amen.

SAINT AMBROSE

LORD Jesus Christ, who didst stretch out thine hands on the cross, and redeem us by thy blood: Forgive me, a sinner, for none of my thoughts are hid from thee. Pardon I ask, pardon I hope for, pardon I trust to have. Thou who art pitiful and merciful: spare me, and forgive.

SAINT AMBROSE

LORD, who hast mercy upon all, take away from me my sins, and mercifully kindle in me the fire of thy Holy Spirit. Take away from me the heart of stone, and give me a heart of flesh, a heart to love and adore thee, a heart to delight in thee, to follow and to enjoy thee, for Christ's sake. Amen.

SAINT AMBROSE

COME, therefore, O Lord Jesus, divest yourself of your garments which you have put on for my sake. Be you naked, that you may clothe us with your mercy. Gird yourself with a towel for our sakes, that you may gird us with your gift of immortality. Pour water into the basin; wash not only our feet but also the head, and not only the footprints of the body, but also of the mind. I wish to put off all the filth of our frailty, so that I, too, may say: "I have put off my garment, how shall I put it on? I have washed my feet, how shall I defile them?"

SAINT AMBROSE

SINCE no one, Lord, can desire more for another than he wishes for himself, I ask you not to separate me when I am dead from those who were so dear to me while I lived.

Lord, I beg you that where I am, they too may be with me. As I have not been able to see much of them here, let me enjoy their company in Heaven forever.

I beseech you, God most high, to grant a speedy resurrection to these children whom I love so much. As the span of their life on earth was cut short, make it up to them by calling them the sooner to eternal life.

SAINT AMBROSE

IF anyone is in danger, the priest is in danger as well; if any sinner's grief is known to him, the priest grieves with him; whatever others suffer, he also bears, and when others are free of the danger that beset them, he is free of it too.

My heart bleeds because a man has been taken from us whose like we can scarcely hope to find. We can but beg and implore you, Lord, on whom alone we can rely, to make him live again in his sons.

You watch over the insignificant, Lord, and keep them humble; protect us, then, whose trust is all in you. Give rest to your servant Theodosius, the rest that you keep for your saints; and may his soul return whence it came. There he will no longer feel death's sting, and he will know that death is not the end of human life but the end of sin. The death he has died is a death to sin, and now there can be no room in him for sin. He will rise again and enter on a higher kind of life.

SAINT AMBROSE

PROTECT, O Lord, those who cry to thee for help. Uphold us in our weakness, and cleanse us from our earthliness: and, whilst we walk in this dying life amidst the shadows of death, do thou ever quicken us with thy light. Vouchsafe in thy mercy to deliver us from all evil, so that we may come to the perfection of all good at last.

SAINT LEO THE GREAT

O Lord: Give to thy people, we pray thee, the spirit of truth and of peace, that they may know thee with all their minds; and that, following with all their hearts after those things which are pleasing to thee, they ever may possess the gifts of thy bountiful goodness.

SAINT LEO THE GREAT

O God, who hast established the foundations of thy Church upon the holy mountains: Grant that she may not be moved by any wiles of error which would fain compass her overthrow, nor may she be shaken by any earthly disquietude, but ever stand firmly upon the ordinances of the apostles, and by their help, be kept in safety.

SAINT LEO THE GREAT

GRANT to us, O Lord, not to mind earthly things, but rather to love heavenly things, that whilst all things around us pass away, we even now may hold fast those things which abide forever.

SAINT LEO THE GREAT

SHOW unto me, O Lord, thy mercy,
And delight my heart with it.
Let me find thee,
Whom so longingly I seek.

See: here is the man
Whom the robbers seized, and mishandled,
And left half dead
On the road to Jericho.
O thou who can
What the kindhearted Samaritan cannot:
Come to my aid!

I am the sheep
Who wandered into the wilderness:
Seek after me,
And bring me home again to thy fold.
Do with me what thou wilt,
That all the days of my life
I may bide by thee, and praise thee,
With all those who art in Heaven with thee
For all of eternity. Amen.

SAINT JEROME

O Christ . . . this I make my only good, this I feel must be held fast, this with my whole heart I long to secure—in all places everywhere and at all times continually, in utterance to tell of thee, and in silence to remember thee. Wherefore—owing all myself to thee, O God most excellent, and all things that are mine—as I began this work from thee, so in finishing it I end to thee; and while I have often prayed thee earnestly, now much more fervently I beseech thee—seeing that in this decrepit age which I now spend I see naught more to be feared but death itself, and cannot readily descry what further I can desire—whichever way thy will inclines, grant me, I pray, a heart unflinching in the face of any sorrow, and make it steadfast by the gift of thy power; that I who long have lived obedient to the laws approved of thee, and seek to win thy promise of salvation, may not too greatly dread the hour of death—now nearer by reason of my advanced age, though every season of life is subject to him. And at the crisis of my changeful life may no idle chances—for these, I trust, may be avoided under thy leadership, O God—distress me with misdoubtful fears: but whatever lot awaits me at my end let hope of beholding thee, O Christ, assuage it, and let all fearful doubts be dispelled by the sure confidence that alike while I am in this mortal body I am thine, since all is thine, and that when released from it I shall be in some part of thy body.

AUSONIUS

O God, our hope, who dost provide for us an endless home; if we by holy prayer and vigil win thy pardon, then, Father, in thy mercy grant us our petitions. Grant us, O Christ, to know thy faultless pattern, O gracious King, thou quickener of thy servants who adore thee—thou, who with the Father, the Unbegotten, art one Majesty most high. Grant through the fellowship of the Comforter a triple stay to aid us, that throngs of worshipers may ceaselessly prolong thy praise: to thee it is they haste fitly to keep vigil. Night shall bring back a light far beyond any taper's ray; night which sends forth a beam in which believers put their trust; night which broods o'er the tasks of the fiery stars. Thou at thy table endest our solemn fasts; thou, who dost promise still increasing blessings, art praised by all with one accord: O thou, our Ruler, give us poor worthless mortals power to express the greatness of the Almighty.

AUSONIUS

O mighty Father of all things; to whom are subject earth, sea, and air, and Hell, and all the expanse of Heaven emblazoned with the Milky Way; before thee tremble the folk guilty of offenses, and contrariwise the blameless company of righteous souls extols thee with prayer and praise. Thou dost reward our course through these few years and the swift close of our frail being with the prize of everlasting life. Thou dost bestow upon mankind the gentle warnings of the Law together with the holy prophets; and, as thou didst pity Adam when beguiled by Eve, on whom the poison seized so that she drew him by her smooth enticements to be the fellow of her transgression, so thou dost keep us, their progeny. Thou, gracious Father, grantest to the world thy Word, who is thy Son, and God, in all things like thee and equal with thee, very God of very God, and living God of the source of life. He, guided by thy behests, added this one gift alone, causing that Spirit which once moved over the face of the deep to quicken our dull members with the cleansing waters of eternal life. Object of our faith, Three, yet One in source, sure hope of our salvation! Grant pardon and bestow on me the gift of life for which I yearn, if I embrace this diversity of Persons united in their powers.

AUSONIUS

MAY the strength of God pilot us.
May the power of God preserve us.
May the wisdom of God instruct us.
May the hand of God protect us.
May the way of God direct us.
May the shield of God defend us.
May the host of God guard us

—Against the snares of the evil ones,
—Against temptations of the world.

May Christ be with us!
May Christ be before us!
May Christ be in us,
Christ be over all!

May thy salvation, Lord,
Always be ours,
This day, O Lord, and evermore.

SAINT PATRICK

I arise today
Through a mighty strength,
Strong virtue of invocation of the Trinity:
  Through belief in the Threeness,
  Through the confession of the Oneness
  Of the Creator of creation.

I arise today
Through a mighty strength:
  The strength of the Incarnation of Christ,
  The strength of Christ in his Baptism,
  The strength of his Crucifixion and his Burial,
  The strength of his Resurrection and his Ascension,
  The strength of his Coming on Judgment Day.

I arise today
Through a mighty strength:
  The virtue of the love of seraphim,
  In the obedience of angels,

In the hope of resurrection unto reward,
By virtue of prayers of patriarchs,
By virtue of predictions of god's prophets,
By virtue of preaching of his apostles,
In virtue of the faith of confessors,
The purity of holy virgins,
And deeds of righteous men.

I arise today
To witness a mighty strength:
The power that created Heaven,
The power that created the light of the sun,
The power that created the brightness of the moon,
The power that created the splendor of fire,
The power that created flashing lightning,
The power that caused the swiftness of winds,
The power that laid the depths of seas,
The power that founded earth's stability,
The power that formed all rocks.

I arise today
Through a mighty strength:
God's power to guide me,
God's might to uphold me,
God's wisdom to teach me,
God's eyes to watch over me,
God's ear to hear me,
God's word to give me speech,
God's hand to guard me,
God's way to lie before me,
God's shield to shelter me,
God's host to secure me:
Against the snares of devils,
Against the seductions of vices,
Against the lusts of nature,
Against everyone who shall wish me ill,
Whether far or near, many or few.

I invoke to my aid
All such virtues of mighty strength:
  Against every merciless, hostile power,
  Which may assail my body and my soul,
  Against the incantations of false prophets, . . .
  Against idolatry's deceits,
  Against the spells of women, druids, and smiths,
  Against all knowledge that blinds the soul of man.

I arise today
Through a mighty strength:
    Christ to protect me today
    Against every poison,
    Against burning,
    Against drowning,
    Against deathly wounds,
    That I may receive abundant reward.

Christ with me, Christ before me,
Christ with me, Christ above,
Christ at my right, Christ at my left,
Christ in the fort, Christ in the chariot seat,
Christ in the poop,
Christ to every eye that sees me,
Christ in every ear that hears me,
That I may receive abundant reward.

I arise today through a mighty strength:
The strength of invocation of the Trinity.
I believe the Trinity in the Unity,
The Creator of the universe.
Amen.

SAINT PATRICK

O my Sovereign Lord: thou who dost give increase to all things: Bless, O God of unbounded greatness, this storehouse with thy right hand.

My storehouse shall be a storehouse of bright testimony, the storehouse which my King shall bless, a storehouse in which plenty shall abound.

The Son of Mary, my beloved One, will bless my storehouse. His is the glory of the whole universe. May that glory ever be multiplied, and be given unto him.

BRIDGID OF ULSTER

I would like the angels of Heaven to be amongst us.
I would like the abundance of peace.

I would like full vessels of charity.
I would like rich treasures of mercy.
I would like cheerfulness to preside over all.

I would like Jesus to be present.
I would like the three Marys of illustrious renown to be with us.
I would like the friends of Heaven to be gathered around us from all parts.

I would like myself to be a rent payer to the Lord; that I should suffer distress, that he would bestow a good blessing upon me.

BRIDGID OF ULSTER

IV. Liturgical Prayers East and West

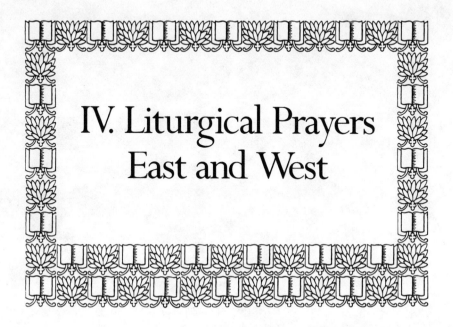

IN fourth- and fifth-century liturgy, with Western and Eastern rites blossoming from their early roots, the early Church achieved a rich and secure expression of corporate or community prayer. The anaphora (the prayer of recollection, recounting the history of salvation and containing the institution of the Eucharist) remains central. It also reflects the relationship of Christian liturgy to its Jewish antecedents, not only synagogue worship but also family and community worship, such as the Passover Seder.

In the first three centuries, much Christian worship was held in people's homes. The Church became far more "public," once the persecutions had ended, and the churches much more grand, in part because the emperor began to commission the construction of mighty cathedrals throughout the empire. All of this had an impact on the liturgy, which itself became more ornate, with prescribed rubrics, elaborate vestments, and extensive calendars replacing the relative informality of earlier worship.

The first complete extant liturgy is the Liturgy of Saint James. To give a sense of how fully developed the traditional liturgy had become by the late fourth century, and to set a frame for the liturgical selections to follow, we present this in its complete (if somewhat later) form, instructions included. The Syriac, Coptic, Ethiopic, and Armenian traditions stem directly from liturgical traditions akin to that represented by the Liturgy of Saint James. The selections we include from these liturgies display the principle of a generally unified liturgy, amidst a diversity of expressions, both formal and linguistic.

Among the Greek liturgies, the anaphora of Saint Basil is the most polished of the early eucharistic prayers and was adapted in the West as well.

In the West, the old Roman canon is said to be of fourth-century origin, and it offered the basic form used in the Roman rite until it was modified in the Second Vatican Council (1962–65). As with so many of these liturgies, the Leonine Sacramentary cannot be dated precisely, but the Gelasian Sacramentary was compiled under Pope Gelasius in 496 and is the oldest extant official book of the Roman rite.

TEN

Prayers from Syriac, Coptic, Ethiopic, and Armenian Liturgies

I.

The Priest.

O Sovereign Lord our God, condemn me not, defiled with a multitude of sins: for, behold, I have come to this thy divine and heavenly mystery, not as being worthy; but looking only to thy goodness, I direct my voice to thee: God be merciful to me, a sinner; I have sinned against Heaven, and before thee, and am unworthy to come into the presence of this thy holy and spiritual table, upon which thy only-begotten Son, and our Lord Jesus Christ, is mystically set forth as a sacrifice for me, a sinner, and stained with every spot. Wherefore I present to thee this supplication and thanksgiving, that thy Spirit the Comforter may be sent down upon me, strengthening and fitting me for this service; and count me worthy to make known without condemnation the Word, delivered from thee by me to the people, in Christ Jesus our Lord, with whom thou art blessed, together with thy all-holy, and good, and quickening, and consubstantial Spirit, now and ever, and to all eternity. Amen.

Prayer of the standing beside the altar.

Glory to the Father, and to the Son, and to the Holy Spirit, the triune light of the Godhead, which is Unity subsisting in Trinity, divided, yet indivisible: for the Trinity is the one God Almighty, whose glory the heavens declare, and the earth his dominion, and the sea his might, and every sentient and intellectual creature at all times proclaims his majesty: for all glory becomes him, and honor and might, greatness and magnificence, now and ever, and to all eternity. Amen.

Prayer of the incense at the beginning.

Sovereign Lord Jesus Christ, O Word of God, who didst freely offer thyself a blameless sacrifice upon the cross to God even the Father, the coal of double nature, that didst touch the lips of the prophet with the tongs, and didst take away his sins, touch also the hearts of us sinners, and purify us from every stain, and present us holy beside thy holy altar, that we may offer thee a sacrifice of praise: and accept from us, thy unprofitable servants, this incense as an odor of a sweet smell, and make fragrant the evil odor of our soul and body, and purify us with the sanctifying power of thy all-holy Spirit: for thou alone art holy, who sanctifiest, and art communicated to the faithful; and glory becomes thee, with thy eternal Father, and thy all-holy, and good, and quickening Spirit, now and ever, and to all eternity. Amen.

Prayer of the commencement.

O beneficent King eternal, and Creator of the universe, receive thy Church, coming unto thee through thy Christ: fulfill to each what is profitable; lead all to perfection, and make us perfectly worthy of the grace of thy sanctification, gathering us together within thy holy Church, which thou hast purchased by the precious blood of thy only-begotten Son, and our Lord and Saviour Jesus Christ, with whom thou art blessed and glorified, together with thy all-holy, and good, and quickening Spirit, now and ever, and to all eternity. Amen.

The Deacon.

Let us again pray to the Lord.

The Priest, prayer of the incense at the entrance of the congregation.

God, who didst accept the gifts of Abel, the sacrifice of Noah and of Abram, the incense of Aaron and Zacharias, accept also from the hand of us sinners this incense for an odor of a sweet smell, and for remission of our sins, and those of all thy people; for blessed art thou, and glory becomes thee, the Father, and the Son, and the Holy Spirit, now and ever.

The Deacon.

Sir, pronounce the blessing.

The Priest prays.

Our Lord and God, Jesus Christ, who through exceeding goodness and love not to be restrained wast crucified, and didst not refuse to be pierced by the spear and nails; who didst provide this mysterious and awful service as an everlasting memorial for us perpetually: bless thy ministry in Christ the God, and bless our entrance, and fully complete the presentation of this our service by thy unutterable compassion, now and ever, and to all eternity. Amen.

The responsive prayer from the Deacon.

The Lord bless us and make us worthy seraphically to offer gifts, and to sing the oft-sung hymn of the divine Trisagion, by the fullness and exceeding abundance of all the perfection of holiness, now and ever.

Then the Deacon begins to sing in the entrance.

Thou who art the only-begotten Son and Word of God, immortal; who didst submit for our salvation to become flesh of the holy God-Mother, and ever-virgin Mary; who didst immutably become man and wast crucified, O Christ our God, and didst by thy death tread death under foot; who art one of the Holy Trinity, glorified together with the Father and the Holy Spirit, save us.

The Priest says this prayer from the gates to the altar.

God Almighty, Lord great in glory, who hast given to us an entrance into the Holy of Holies, through the sojourning among men of thy only-begotten Son, our Lord, and God, and Saviour Jesus Christ, we supplicate and invoke thy goodness, since we are fearful and trembling when about to stand at thy holy altar; send forth upon us, O God, thy good grace, and sanctify our souls, and bodies, and spirits, and turn our thoughts to piety, in order that with a pure conscience we may bring unto thee gifts, offerings, and fruits for the remission of our transgressions, and for the propitiation of all thy people, by the grace and mercies and loving kindness of thy only-begotten Son, with whom thou art blessed to all eternity. Amen.

After the approach to the altar, the Priest says:

Peace be to all.

The People.

And to thy spirit.

The Priest.

The Lord bless us all, and sanctify us for the entrance and celebration of the divine and pure mysteries, giving rest to the blessed souls among the good and just, by his grace and loving kindness, now and ever, and to all eternity. Amen.

Then the Deacon says the bidding prayer.

In peace let us beseech the Lord.

For the peace that is from above, and for God's love to man, and for the salvation of our souls, let us beseech the Lord.

For the peace of the whole world, for the unity of all the holy churches of God, let us beseech the Lord.

For the remission of our sins, and forgiveness of our transgressions, and for our deliverance from all tribulation, wrath, danger, and distress, and from the uprising of our enemies, let us beseech the Lord.

Then the Singers sing the Trisagion Hymn.

Holy God, holy Mighty, holy Immortal, have mercy upon us.

Then the Priest prays, bowing.

O compassionate and merciful, long-suffering and very gracious and true God, look from thy prepared dwelling place, and hear us, thy suppliants, and deliver us from every temptation of the Devil and of man; withhold not thy aid from us, nor bring on us chastisements too heavy for our strength: for we are unable to overcome what is opposed to us; but thou art able, Lord, to save us from everything that is against us. Save us, O God, from the difficulties of this world, according to thy goodness, in order that, having drawn nigh with a pure conscience to thy holy altar, we may send up to thee without condemnation the blessed hymn Trisagion, together with the heavenly powers, and that, having performed the service, well pleasing to thee and divine, we may be counted worthy of eternal life.

(Aloud.)

Because thou art holy, Lord our God, and dwellest and abidest in holy places, we send up the praise and the hymn Trisagion to thee, the Father, and the Son, and the Holy Spirit, now and ever, and to all eternity.

The People.

Amen.

The Priest.

Peace be to all.

The People.

And to thy spirit.

The Singers.

Alleluia.

Then there are read in order the holy oracles of the Old Testament, and of the prophets; and the incarnation of the Son of God is set forth, and his sufferings and resurrection from the dead, his ascension into Heaven, and his second appearing with glory; and this takes place daily in the holy and divine service.

After the reading and instruction the Deacon says:

Let us all say, Lord, be merciful.

Lord Almighty, the God of our fathers;

We beseech thee, hear us.

For the peace which is from above, and for the salvation of our souls;

Let us beseech the Lord.

For the peace of the whole world, and the unity of all the holy churches of God;

Let us beseech the Lord.

For the salvation and help of all the Christ-loving people;

We beseech thee, hear us.

For our deliverance from all tribulation, wrath, danger, distress, from captivity, bitter death, and from our iniquities;

We beseech thee, hear us.

For the people standing round, and waiting for the rich and plenteous mercy that is from thee;

We beseech thee, be merciful and gracious.

Save thy people, O Lord, and bless thine inheritance.

Visit thy world in mercy and compassion.

Exalt the horn of Christians by the power of the precious and quickening cross.

We beseech thee, most merciful Lord, hear us praying to thee, and have mercy upon us.

The People (thrice).

Lord, have mercy upon us.

The Deacon.

For the remission of our sins, and forgiveness of our transgressions, and for our deliverance from all tribulation, wrath, danger, and distress, let us beseech the Lord.

Let us all entreat from the Lord, that we may pass the whole day, perfect, holy, peaceful, and without sin.

Let us entreat from the Lord a messenger of peace, a faithful guide, a guardian of our souls and bodies.

Let us entreat from the Lord forgiveness and remission of our sins and transgressions.

Let us entreat from the Lord the things which are good and proper for our souls, and peace for the world.

Let us entreat from the Lord, that we may spend the remaining period of our life in peace and health.

Let us entreat that the close of our lives may be Christian, without pain and without shame, and a good plea at the dread and awful judgment seat of Christ.

The Priest.

For thou art the Gospel and the Light, Saviour and Keeper of our souls and bodies, God, and thy only-begotten Son, and thy all-holy Spirit, now and ever.

The People.

Amen.

The Priest.

God, who hast taught us thy divine and saving oracles, enlighten the souls of us sinners for the comprehension of the things which have been before spoken, so that we may not only be seen to be hearers of spiritual things, but also doers of good deeds, striving after guileless faith, blameless life, and pure conversation.

(Aloud.)

In Christ Jesus our Lord, with whom thou art blessed, together with thy all-holy, good, and quickening Spirit, now and always, and forever.

The People.

Amen.

The Priest.

Peace be to all.

The People.

And to thy spirit.

The Deacon.

Let us bow our heads to the Lord.

The People.

To thee, Lord.

The Priest prays, saying:

O Sovereign Giver of life, and Provider of good things, who didst give to mankind the blessed hope of eternal life, our Lord Jesus Christ, count us worthy in holiness, and perfect this thy divine service to the enjoyment of future blessedness.

(Aloud.)

So that, guarded by thy power at all times, and led into the light of truth, we may send up the praise and the thanksgiving to thee, the Father, the Son, and the Holy Spirit, now and ever.

The People.

Amen.

The Deacon.

Let none remain of the catechumens, none of the unbaptized, none of those who are unable to join with us in prayer. Look at one another. The door.

All erect: let us again pray to the Lord.

II.

The Priest says the prayer of incense.

Sovereign Almighty, King of Glory, who knowest all things before their creation, manifest thyself to us calling upon thee at this holy hour, and redeem us from the shame of our transgressions; cleanse our mind and our thoughts from impure desires, from worldly deceit, from all influence of the Devil; and accept from the hands of us sinners this incense, as thou didst accept the offering of Abel, and Noah, and Aaron, and Samuel, and of all thy saints, guarding us from everything evil, and preserving us for continually pleasing, and worshiping, and glorifying thee, the Father, and thy only-begotten Son, and thy all-holy Spirit, now and always, and forever.

And the Readers begin the Cherubic Hymn.

Let all mortal flesh be silent, and stand with fear and trembling, and meditate nothing earthly within itself:

For the King of kings and Lord of lords, Christ our God, comes forward to be sacrificed, and to be given for food to the faithful; and the bands of angels go before him with every power and dominion, the many-eyed cherubim, and the six-winged seraphim, covering their faces, and crying aloud the hymn, Alleluia, Alleluia, Alleluia.

The Priest, bringing in the holy gifts, says this prayer:

O God, our God, who didst send forth the heavenly bread, the food of the whole world, our Lord Jesus Christ, to be a Saviour, and Redeemer, and Benefactor, blessing and sanctifying us, do thou thyself bless this offering, and graciously receive it to thy altar above the skies:

Remember in thy goodness and love those who have brought it, and those for whom they have brought it, and preserve us without condemnation in the service of thy divine mysteries: for hallowed and glorified is thy all-honored and great name, Father, the Son, and Holy Spirit, now and ever, and to all eternity.

The Priest.

Peace be to all.

The Deacon.

Sir, pronounce the blessing.

The Priest.

Blessed be God, who blesseth and sanctifieth us all at the presentation of the divine and pure mysteries, and giveth rest to the blessed souls among the holy and just, now and always, and to all eternity.

The Deacon.

Let us attend in wisdom.

The Priest begins.

I believe in one God, Father Almighty, Maker of Heaven and earth, and in one Lord Jesus Christ, the Son of God: *and the rest of the Creed.*

Then he prays, bowing his neck.

God and Sovereign of all, make us, who are unworthy, worthy of this hour, lovers of mankind; that being pure from all deceit and all hypocrisy, we may be united with one another by the bond of peace and love, being confirmed by the sanctification of thy divine knowledge through thine only-begotten Son, our Lord and Saviour Jesus Christ, with whom thou art blessed, together with thy all-holy, and good, and quickening Spirit, now and ever, and to all eternity. Amen.

The Deacon.

Let us stand well, let us stand reverently, let us stand in the fear of God, and with compunction of heart. In peace let us pray to the Lord.

The Priest.

For God of peace, mercy, love, compassion, and loving kindness art thou, and thine only-begotten Son, and thine all-holy Spirit, now and ever.

The People.

Amen.

The Priest.

Peace be to all.

The People.

And to thy spirit.

The Deacon.

Let us salute one another with a holy kiss. Let us bow our heads to the Lord.

The Priest bows, saying this prayer:

Only Lord and merciful God, on those who are bowing their necks before thy holy altar, and seeking the spiritual gifts that come from thee, send forth thy good grace; and bless us all with every spiritual blessing, that cannot be taken from us, thou, who dwellest on high, and hast regard unto things that are lowly.

(Aloud.)

For worthy of praise and worship and most glorious is thy all-holy name, Father and Son and Holy Spirit, now and always, and to all eternity.

The Deacon.

Sir, pronounce the blessing.

The Priest.

The Lord will bless us, and minister with us all by his grace and loving kindness.

And again.

The Lord will bless us, and make us worthy to stand at his holy altar, at all times, now and always, and forever.

And again.

Blessed be God, who blesseth and sanctifieth us all in our attendance upon, and service of, his pure mysteries, now and always, and forever.

The Deacon makes the Universal Litany.

In peace let us pray to the Lord.

The People.

O Lord, have mercy.

The Deacon.

Save us, have mercy upon us, pity and keep us, O God, by thy grace.

For the peace that is from above, and the loving kindness of God, and the salvation of our souls;

Let us beseech the Lord.

For the peace of the whole world, and the unity of all the holy churches of God;

Let us beseech the Lord.

For those who bear fruit, and labor honorably in the holy churches of God; for those who remember the poor, the widows and the orphans, the strangers and needy ones; and for those who have requested us to mention them in our prayers;

Let us beseech the Lord.

For those who are in old age and infirmity, for the sick and suffering, and those who are troubled by unclean spirits, for their speedy cure from God and their salvation;

Let us beseech the Lord.

For those who are passing their days in virginity, and celibacy, and discipline, and for those in holy matrimony; and for the holy fathers and brethren agonizing in mountains and dens, and caves of the earth;

Let us beseech the Lord.

For Christians sailing, traveling, living among strangers, and for our brethren in captivity, in exile, in prison, and in bitter slavery, their peaceful return;

Let us beseech the Lord.

For the remission of our sins, and forgiveness of our transgressions, and for our deliverance from all tribulation, wrath, danger, and constraint, and uprising against us of enemies;

Let us beseech the Lord.

For favorable weather, peaceful showers, beneficent dews, abundance of fruits, the perfect close of a good season, and for the crown of the year;

Let us beseech the Lord.

For our fathers and brethren present, and praying with us in this holy hour, and at every season, their zeal, labor, and earnestness;

Let us beseech the Lord.

For every Christian soul in tribulation and distress, and needing the mercy and succor of God; for the return of the erring, the health of the sick, the deliverance of the captives, the rest of the fathers and brethren that have fallen asleep aforetime;

Let us beseech the Lord.

For the hearing and acceptance of our prayer before God, and the sending down on us his rich mercies and compassion;

Let us beseech the Lord.

And for the offered, precious, heavenly, unutterable, pure, glorious, dread, awful, divine gifts, and the salvation of the priest who stands by and offers them;

Let us offer supplication to God the Lord.

The People.

O Lord, have mercy.

(Thrice.)

Then the Priest makes the sign of the cross on the gifts and, standing, speaks separately thus:

Glory to God in the highest, and on earth peace, good will among men, etc.

(Thrice.)

Lord, thou wilt open my lips, and my mouth shall show forth thy praise.

(Thrice.)

Let my mouth be filled with thy praise, O Lord, that I may tell of thy glory, of thy majesty, all the day.

(Thrice.)

Of the Father. Amen. And of the Son. Amen. And of the Holy Spirit. Amen. Now and always, and to all eternity. Amen.

And bowing to this side and to that, he says:

Magnify the Lord with me, and let us exalt his name together.

And they answer, bowing:

The Holy Ghost shall come upon thee, and the power of the Highest shall overshadow thee.

Then the Priest, at great length:

O Sovereign Lord, who hast visited us in compassion and mercies, and hast freely given to us, thy humble and sinful and unworthy servants, boldness to stand at thy holy altar, and to offer to thee this dread and bloodless sacrifice for our sins, and for the errors of the people, look upon me thy unprofitable servant, and blot out my transgressions for thy compassion's sake; and purify my lips and heart from all pollution of flesh and spirit; and remove from me every shameful and foolish thought, and fit me by the power of thy all-holy Spirit for this service; and receive me graciously by thy goodness as I draw nigh to thy altar.

And be pleased, O Lord, that these gifts brought by our hands may be acceptable, stooping to my weakness; and cast me not away from thy presence, and abhor not my unworthiness; but pity me according to thy great mercy, and according to the multitude of thy mercies pass by my transgressions, that, having come before thy glory without condemnation, I may be counted worthy of the protection of thy only-begotten Son, and of the illumination of thy all-holy Spirit, that I may not be as a slave of sin cast out, but as thy servant may find grace and mercy and forgiveness of sins before thee, both in the world that now is and in that which is to come.

I beseech thee, Almighty Sovereign, all-powerful Lord, hear my prayer; for thou art he who workest all in all, and we all seek in all things the help and succor that come from thee and thy only-begotten Son, and the good and quickening and consubstantial Spirit, now and ever.

O God, who through thy great and unspeakable love didst send forth thy only-begotten Son into the world, in order that he might turn back the lost sheep, turn not away us sinners, laying hold of thee by this dread and bloodless sacrifice; for we trust not in our own righteousness, but in thy good mercy, by which thou purchasest our race.

We entreat and beseech thy goodness that it may not be for condemnation to thy people that this mystery for salvation has been administered by us, but for remission of sins, for renewal of souls and bodies, for the well-pleasing of thee, God and Father, in the mercy and love of thy only-begotten Son, with whom thou art blessed, together with thy all-holy and good and quickening Spirit, now and always, and forever.

O Lord God, who didst create us, and bring us into life, who hast shown to us ways to salvation, who hast granted to us a revelation of heavenly mysteries, and hast appointed us to this ministry in the power of thy all-holy Spirit, grant, O Sovereign, that we may become servants of thy new testament, ministers of thy pure mysteries, and receive us as we draw near to thy holy altar, according to the greatness of thy mercy, that we may become worthy of offering to thee gifts and sacrifices for our transgressions and for those of the people; and grant to us, O Lord, with all fear and a pure conscience to offer to thee this spiritual and bloodless sacrifice, and graciously receiving it unto thy holy and spiritual altar above the skies for an odor of a sweet spiritual smell, send down in answer on us the grace of thy all-holy Spirit.

And, O God, look upon us, and have regard to this our reasonable service, and accept it, as thou didst accept the gifts of Abel, the sacrifices of Noah, the priestly offices of Moses and Aaron, the peace offerings of Samuel, the repentance of David, the incense of Zacharias. As thou didst accept from the hand of thy apostles this true service, so accept also in thy goodness from the hands of us sinners these offered gifts; and grant that our offering may be acceptable, sanctified by the Holy Spirit, as a propitiation for our transgressions and the errors of the people; and for the rest of the souls that have fallen asleep aforetime; that we also, thy humble, sinful, and unworthy servants, being counted worthy without guile to serve thy holy altar, may receive the reward of faithful and wise stewards, and may find grace and mercy in the terrible day of thy just and good retribution.

Prayer of the veil.

We thank thee, O Lord our God, that thou hast given us boldness for the entrance of thy holy places, which thou hast renewed to us as a new and living way through the veil of the flesh of thy Christ. We therefore, being counted worthy to enter into the place of the tabernacle of thy glory, and to be within the veil, and to behold the Holy of Holies, cast ourselves down before thy goodness:

Lord, have mercy on us: since we are full of fear and trembling, when about to stand at thy holy altar, and to offer this dread and bloodless sacrifice for our own sins and for the errors of the people: send forth, O God, thy good grace, and sanctify our souls, and bodies, and spirits; and turn our thoughts to holiness, that with a pure conscience we may bring to thee a peace offering, the sacrifice of praise:

(Aloud.)

By the mercy and loving kindness of thy only-begotten Son, with whom thou art blessed, together with thy all-holy, and good, and quickening Spirit, now and always.

The People.

Amen.

The Priest.

Peace be to all.

The Deacon.

Let us stand reverently, let us stand in the fear of God, and with contrition: let us attend to the holy communion service, to offer peace to God.

The People.

The offering of peace, the sacrifice of praise.

The Priest. [A veil is now withdrawn from the oblation of bread and wine.]

And, uncovering the veils that darkly invest in symbol this sacred ceremonial, do thou reveal it clearly to us: fill our intellectual vision with absolute light, and having purified our poverty from every pollution of flesh and spirit, make it worthy of this dread and awful approach: for Thou art an all-merciful and gracious God, and we send up the praise and the thanksgiving to thee, Father, Son, and Holy Spirit, now, and always, and forever.

III.

THE ANAPHORA

Then he says aloud:

The love of the Lord and Father, the grace of the Lord and Son, and the fellowship and the gift of the Holy Spirit, be with us all.

The People.

And with thy spirit.

The Priest.

Let us lift up our minds and our hearts.

The People.

It is becoming and right.

Then the Priest prays.

Verily it is becoming and right, proper and due to praise thee, to sing of thee, to bless thee, to worship thee, to glorify thee, to give thee thanks, Maker of every creature visible and invisible, the treasure of eternal good things, the fountain of life and immortality, God and Lord of all:

Whom the heavens of heavens praise, and all the host of them; the sun, and the moon, and all the choir of the stars; earth, sea, and all that is in them; Jerusalem, the heavenly assembly, and church of the firstborn that are written in heaven; spirits of just men and of prophets; souls of martyrs and of apostles; angels, archangels, thrones, dominions, principalities, and authorities, and dread powers; and the many-eyed cherubim, and the six-winged seraphim, which cover their faces with two wings, their feet with two, and with two they fly, crying one to another with unresting lips, with unceasing praises:

(Aloud.)

With loud voice singing the victorious hymn of thy majestic glory, crying aloud, praising, shouting, and saying:

The People.

Holy, holy, holy, O Lord of Sabaoth, the heaven and the earth are full of thy glory. Hosanna in the highest; blessed is he that cometh in the name of the Lord. Hosanna in the highest.

The Priest, making the sign of the cross on the gifts, says:

Holy art thou, King of eternity, and Lord and Giver of all holiness; holy also thy only-begotten Son, our Lord Jesus Christ, by whom thou hast made all things; holy also thy Holy Spirit, which searches all things, even thy deep things, O God: holy art thou, almighty, all-powerful, good, dread, merciful, most compassionate to thy creatures;

who didst make man from earth after thine own image and likeness; who didst give him the joy of Paradise; and when he transgressed thy commandment, and fell away, didst not disregard nor desert him, O Good One, but didst chasten him as a merciful father, call him by the law, instruct him by the prophets; and afterwards didst send forth thine only-begotten Son himself, our Lord Jesus Christ, into the world, that he by his coming might renew and restore thy image;

Who, having descended from heaven, and become flesh of the Holy Spirit and Virgin Godmother Mary, and having sojourned among men, fulfilled the dispensation for the salvation of our race; and being about to endure his voluntary and life-giving death by the cross, he the sinless for us the sinners, in the night in which he was betrayed, nay, rather delivered himself up for the life and salvation of the world.

Then the Priest holds the bread in his hand, and says:

Having taken the bread in his holy and pure and blameless and immortal hands, lifting up his eyes to heaven, and showing it to thee, his God and Father, he gave thanks, and hallowed, and brake, and gave it to us, his disciples and apostles, saying:

The Deacons say:

For the remission of sins and life everlasting.

Then he says aloud:

Take, eat: this is my body, broken for you, and given for remission of sins.

The People.

Amen.

Then he takes the cup, and says:

In like manner, after supper, he took the cup, and having mixed wine and water, lifting up his eyes to Heaven, and presenting it to thee, his God and Father, he gave thanks, and hallowed and blessed it, and filled it with the Holy Spirit, and gave it to us, his disciples, saying, Drink ye all of it; this is my blood of the new testament, shed for you and many, and distributed for the remission of sins.

The People.

Amen.

The Priest.

This do in remembrance of me; for as often as ye eat this bread, and drink this cup, ye do show forth the Lord's death, and confess his resurrection, till he come.

The Deacons say:

We believe and confess:

The People.

We show forth thy death, O Lord, and confess thy resurrection.

The Priest (Oblation).

Remembering, therefore, his life-giving sufferings, his saving cross, his death and his burial, and resurrection from the dead on the third day, and his ascension into Heaven, and sitting at the right hand of thee, our God and Father, and his second glorious and awful appearing, when he shall come with glory to judge the quick and the dead, and render to everyone according to his works; even we, sinful men, offer unto thee, O Lord, this dread and bloodless sacrifice, praying that thou wilt not deal with us after our sins, nor reward us according to our iniquities;

But that thou, according to thy mercy and thy unspeakable loving kindness, passing by and blotting out the handwriting against us thy suppliants, wilt grant to us thy heavenly and eternal gifts (which eye hath not seen, and ear hath not heard, and which have not entered into the heart of man) that thou hast prepared, O God, for those who love thee; and reject not, O loving Lord, the people for my sake, or for my sin's sake:

Then he says, thrice:

For thy people and thy Church supplicate thee.

The People.

Have mercy on us, O Lord our God, Father Almighty.

Again the Priest says (Invocation):

Have mercy upon us, O God Almighty.

Have mercy upon us, O God our Saviour.

Have mercy upon us, O God, according to thy great mercy, and send forth on us, and on these offered gifts, thy all-holy Spirit.

Then, bowing his neck, he says:

The sovereign and quickening Spirit, that sits upon the throne with thee, our God and Father, and with thy only-begotten Son, reigning with thee; the consubstantial and co-eternal; that spoke in the law and in the prophets, and in thy New Testament; that descended in the form of a dove on our Lord Jesus Christ at the river Jordan, and abode on him; that descended on thy apostles in the form of tongues of fire in the upper room of the holy and glorious Zion on the day of Pentecost: this thine all-holy Spirit, send down, O Lord, upon us, and upon these offered holy gifts;

And rising up, he says aloud:

That coming, by his holy and good and glorious appearing, he may sanctify this bread, and make it the holy body of thy Christ.

The People.

Amen.

The Priest.

And this cup the precious blood of thy Christ.

The People.

Amen.

The Priest by himself standing.

That they may be to all that partake of them for remission of sins, and for life everlasting, for the sanctification of souls and of bodies, for bearing the fruit of good works, for the stablishing of thy holy catholic Church, which thou hast founded on the Rock of Faith, that the gates of Hell may not prevail against it; delivering it from all heresy and scandals, and from those who work iniquity, keeping it till the fullness of the time.

And having bowed, he says:

We present them to thee also, O Lord, for the holy places, which thou hast glorified by the divine appearing of thy Christ, and by the visitation of thy all-holy Spirit; especially for the glorious Zion, the mother of all the churches; and for thy holy, catholic, and apostolic Church throughout the world: even now, O Lord, bestow upon her the rich gifts of thy all-holy Spirit.

Remember also, O Lord, our holy fathers and brethren in it, and the bishops in all the world, who rightly divide the word of thy truth.

Remember also, O Lord, every city and country, and those of the true faith dwelling in them, their peace and security.

Remember, O Lord, Christians sailing, traveling, sojourning in strange lands; our fathers and brethren, who are in bonds, prison, captivity, and exile; who are in mines, and under torture, and in bitter slavery.

Remember, O Lord, the sick and afflicted, and those troubled by unclean spirits, their speedy healing from thee, O God, and their salvation.

Remember, O Lord, every Christian soul in affliction and distress, needing thy mercy and succor, O God; and the return of the erring.

Remember, O Lord, our fathers and brethren, toiling hard, and ministering unto us, for thy holy name's sake.

Remember all, O Lord, for good: have mercy on all, O Lord, be reconciled to us all: give peace to the multitudes of thy people: put away scandals: bring wars to an end: make the uprising of heresies to cease: grant thy peace and thy love to us, O God our Saviour, the hope of all the ends of the earth.

Remember, O Lord, favorable weather, peaceful showers, beneficent dews, abundance of fruits, and to crown the year with thy goodness; for the eyes of all wait on thee, and thou givest their food in due season: thou openest thy hand, and fillest every living thing with gladness.

Remember, O Lord, those who bear fruit, and labor honorably in the holy of thy Church; and those who forget not the poor, the widows, the orphans, the strangers, and the needy; and all who have desired us to remember them in our prayers.

Moreover, O Lord, be pleased to remember those who have brought these offerings this day to thy holy altar, and for what each one has brought them or with what mind, and those persons who have just now been mentioned to thee.

Remember, O Lord, according to the multitude of thy mercy and compassion, me also, thy humble and unprofitable servant; and the deacons who surround thy holy altar, and graciously give them a blameless life, keep their ministry undefiled, and purchase for them a good degree, that we may find mercy and grace, with all the saints that have been well pleasing to thee since the world began, to generation and generation—grandsires, sires, patriarchs, prophets, apostles, martyrs, confessors, teachers, saints, and every just spirit made perfect in the faith of thy Christ.

Hail, Mary, highly favored: the Lord is with thee; blessed art thou among women, and blessed the fruit of thy womb, for thou didst bear the Saviour of our souls.

The Deacons.

Remember us, O Lord God.

The Priest, bowing, says:

Remember, O Lord God, the spirits and all flesh, of whom we have made mention, and of whom we have not made mention, who are of the true faith, from righteous Abel unto this day: unto them do thou give rest there in the land of the living, in thy kingdom, in the joy of paradise, in the bosom of Abraham, and of Isaac, and of Jacob, our holy fathers; whence pain, and grief, and lamentation have fled: there the light of thy countenance looks upon them, and enlightens them forever.

Make the end of our lives Christian, acceptable, blameless, and peaceful, O Lord, gathering us together, O Lord, under the feet of thine elect, when thou wilt, and as thou wilt; only without shame and transgressions, through thy only-begotten Son, our Lord and God and Saviour Jesus Christ: for he is the only sinless one who hath appeared on the earth.

The Deacon.

And let us pray:

For the peace and establishing of the whole world, and of the holy churches of God, and for the purposes for which each one made his offering, or according to the desire he has: and for the people standing round, and for all men, and all women:

The People.

And for all men and all women. (Amen.)

The Priest says aloud:

Wherefore, both to them and to us, do thou in thy goodness and love:

The People.

Forgive, remit, pardon, O God, our transgressions, voluntary and involuntary: in deed and in word: in knowledge and in ignorance: by night and by day: in thought and intent: in thy goodness and love, forgive us them all.

The Priest.

Through the grace and compassion and love of thy only-begotten Son, with whom thou art blessed and glorified, together with the all-holy, and good, and quickening Spirit, now and ever, and to all eternity.

The People.

Amen.

The Priest.

Peace be to all:

The People.

And to thy spirit.

The Deacon.

Again, and continually, in peace let us pray to the Lord.

For the gifts to the Lord God presented and sanctified, precious, heavenly, unspeakable, pure, glorious, dread, awful, divine;

Let us pray.

That the Lord our God, having graciously received them to his altar that is holy and above the heavens, rational and spiritual, for the odor of a sweet spiritual saviour, may send down in answer upon us the divine grace and the gift of the all-holy Spirit;

Let us pray.

Having prayed for the unity of the faith, and the communion of his all-holy and adorable Spirit;

Let us commend ourselves and one another, and our whole life, to Christ our God:

The People.

Amen.

The Priest prays.

God and Father of our Lord and God and Saviour Jesus Christ, the glorious Lord, the blessed Essence, the bounteous Goodness, the God and Sovereign of all, who art blessed to all eternity, who sittest upon the cherubim, and art glorified by the seraphim, before whom stand thousand thousands and ten thousand times ten thousand hosts of angels and archangels: Thou hast accepted the gifts, offerings, and fruits brought unto thee as an odor of a sweet spiritual smell, and hast been pleased to sanctify them, and make them perfect, O good One, by the grace of thy Christ, and by the presence of thy all-holy Spirit.

Sanctify also, O Lord, our souls, and bodies, and spirits, and touch our understandings, and search our consciences, and cast out from us every evil imagination, every impure feeling, every base desire, every unbecoming thought, all envy, and vanity, and hypocrisy, all lying, all deceit, every worldly affection, all covetousness, all vainglory, all indifference, all vice, all passion, all anger, all malice, all blasphemy, every motion of the flesh and spirit that is not in accordance with thy holy will:

Aloud.

And count us worthy, O loving Lord, with boldness, without condemnation, in a pure heart, with a contrite spirit, with unshamed face, with sanctified lips, to dare to call upon thee, the holy God, Father in Heaven, and to say,

The People.

Our Father, which art in Heaven: hallowed be thy name; *and so on to the doxology.*

The Priest, bowing, says (the Embolism):

And lead us not into temptation, Lord, Lord of Hosts, who knowest our frailty, but deliver us from the evil one and his works, and from all his malice and craftiness, for the sake of thy holy name, which has been placed upon our humility:

(Aloud.)

For thine is the kingdom, the power, and the glory, Father, Son, and Holy Spirit, now and forever.

The People.

Amen.

The Priest.

Peace be to all.

The People.

And to thy spirit.

The Deacon.

Let us bow our heads to the Lord.

The People.

To thee, O Lord.

The Priest prays, speaking thus:

To thee, O Lord, we thy servants have bowed our heads before thy holy altar, waiting for the rich mercies that are from thee.

Send forth upon us, O Lord, thy plenteous grace and thy blessing; and sanctify our souls, bodies, and spirits, that we may become worthy communicants and partakers of thy holy mysteries, to the forgiveness of sins and life everlasting:

(Aloud.)

For adorable and glorified art thou, our God, and thy only-begotten Son, and thy all-holy Spirit, now and ever.

The People.

Amen.

The Priest says aloud:

And the grace and the mercies of the holy and consubstantial, and uncreated, and adorable Trinity, shall be with us all.

The People.

And with thy spirit.

The Deacon.

In the fear of God, let us attend.

The Priest says secretly:

O holy Lord, that abidest in holy places, sanctify us by the word of thy grace, and by the visitation of thy all-holy Spirit: for thou, O Lord, hast said, ye will be holy, for I am holy. O Lord our God, incomprehensible Word of God, one in substance with the Father and the Holy Spirit, co-eternal and indivisible, accept the pure hymn, in thy holy and bloodless sacrifices; with the cherubim, and seraphim, and from me, a sinful man, crying and saying:

He takes up the gifts and saith aloud:

The holy things unto holy.

The People.

One only is holy, one Lord Jesus Christ, to the glory of God the Father, to whom be glory to all eternity.

The Deacon.

For the remission of our sins, and the propitiation of our souls, and for every soul in tribulation and distress, needing the mercy and succor of God, and for the return of the erring, the healing of the sick, the deliverance of the captives, the rest of our fathers and brethren, who have fallen asleep aforetime;

Let us say fervently, Lord, have mercy:

The People (twelve times).

Lord, have mercy.

Then the Priest breaks the bread, and holds the half in his right hand, and the half in his left, and dips that in his right hand in the chalice, saying:

The union of the all-holy body and precious blood of our Lord and God and Saviour, Jesus Christ.

Then he makes the sign of the cross on that in his left hand: then with that which has been signed the other half: then forthwith he begins to divide, and before all to give to each chalice a single piece, saying:

It has been made one, and sanctified, and perfected, in the name of the Father, and of the Son, and of the Holy Spirit, now and ever.

And when he makes the sign of the cross on the bread, he says:

Behold the Lamb of God, the Son of the Father, that taketh away the sin of the world, sacrificed for the life and salvation of the world.

And when he gives a single piece to each chalice, he says:

A holy portion of Christ, full of grace and truth, of the Father, and of the Holy Spirit, to whom be the glory and the power to all eternity.

The he begins to divide, and to say:

The Lord is my Shepherd, I shall not want. In green pastures, *and so on.*

Then,

I will bless the Lord at all times, *and so on.*

Then,

I will extol thee, my God, O King, *and so on.*

Then,

O praise the Lord, all ye nations, *and so on.*

The Deacon.

Sir, pronounce the blessing.

The Priest.

The Lord will bless us, and keep us without condemnation for the communion of his pure gifts, now and always, and forever.

And when they have filled, the Deacon says:

Sir, pronounce the blessing.

The Priest says:

The Lord will bless us, and make us worthy with the pure touchings of our fingers to take the live coal, and place it upon the mouths of the faithful for the purification and renewal of their souls and bodies, now and always.

Then,

O taste and see that the Lord is good; who is parted and not divided; distributed to the faithful and not expended; for the remission of sins, and the life everlasting; now and always, and forever.

The Deacon.

In the peace of Christ, let us sing:

The Singers.

O taste and see that the Lord is good.

The Priest says the prayer before the communion.

O Lord our God, the heavenly Bread, the Life of the universe, I have sinned against Heaven, and before thee, and am not worthy to partake of thy pure mysteries; but as a merciful God, make me worthy by thy grace, without condemnation to partake of thy holy body and precious blood, for the remission of sins, and life everlasting.

Then he distributes to the clergy; and when the deacons take the disks and the chalices for distribution to the people, the Deacon, who takes the first disk, says:

Sir, pronounce the blessing.

The Priest replies:

Glory to God who has sanctified and is sanctifying us all.

The Deacon says:

Be thou exalted, O God, over the heavens, and thy glory over all the earth, and thy kingdom endureth to all eternity.

And when the Deacon is about to put it on the side table, the Priest says:

Blessed be the name of the Lord our God forever.

The Deacon.

In the fear of God, and in faith and love, draw nigh.

The People.

Blessed is he that cometh in the name of the Lord.

And again, when he sets down the disk upon the side table, he says:

Sir, pronounce the blessing.

The Priest.

Save thy people, O God, and bless thine inheritance.

The Priest again.

Glory to our God, who has sanctified us all.

And when he has put the chalice back on the holy table, the Priest says:

Blessed be the name of the Lord to all eternity.

The Deacons and the People say:

Fill our mouths with thy praise, O Lord, and fill our lips with joy, that we may sing of thy glory, of thy greatness all the day.

And again:

We render thanks to thee, Christ our God, that thou hast made us worthy to partake of thy body and blood, for the remission of sins, and for life everlasting. Do thou, in thy goodness and love, keep us, we pray thee, without condemnation.

The prayer of incense at the last entrance.

We render thanks to thee, the Saviour and God of all, for all the good things thou hast given us, and for the participation of thy holy and pure mysteries, and we offer to thee this incense, praying: Keep us under the shadow of thy wings, and count us worthy till our last breath to partake of thy holy rites for the sanctification of our souls and bodies, for the inheritance of the kingdom of heaven: for thou, O God, art our sanctification, and we send up praise and thanksgiving to thee, Father, Son, and Holy Spirit.

The Deacon begins in the entrance.

Glory to thee, glory to thee, glory to thee, O Christ the King, only-begotten Word of the Father, that thou hast counted us, thy sinful and unworthy servants, worthy to enjoy thy pure mysteries for the remission of sins, and for life everlasting: glory to thee.

And when he has made the entrance, the Deacon begins to speak thus:

Again and again, and at all times, in peace, let us beseech the Lord.

That the participation of his holy rites may be to us for the turning away from every wicked thing, for our support on the journey to life everlasting, for the communion and gift of the Holy Spirit;

Let us pray.

The Priest prays.

Commemorating our all-holy, pure, most glorious, blessed Lady, the God-Mother and Ever-Virgin Mary, and all the saints that have been well pleasing to thee since the world began, let us devote ourselves, and one another, and our whole life, to Christ our God:

The People.

To thee, O Lord.

The Priest.

O God, who through thy great and unspeakable love didst condescend to the weakness of thy servants, and hast counted us worthy to partake of this heavenly table, condemn not us sinners for the participation of thy pure mysteries; but keep us, O good One, in the sanctification of thy Holy Spirit, that being made holy, we may find part and inheritance with all thy saints that have been well pleasing to thee since the world began, in the light of thy countenance, through the mercy of thy only-begotten Son, our Lord and God and Saviour Jesus Christ, with whom thou art blessed, together with thy all-holy, and good, and quickening Spirit: for blessed and glorified is thy all-precious and glorious name, Father, Son, and Holy Spirit, now and ever, and to all eternity.

The People.

Amen.

The Priest.

Peace be to all.

The People.

And to thy spirit.

The Deacon.

Let us bow our heads to the Lord.

The Priest.

O God, great and marvelous, look upon thy servants, for we have bowed our heads to thee. Stretch forth thy hand, strong and full of blessings, and bless thy people. Keep thine inheritance, that always and at all times we may glorify thee, our only living and true God, the holy and consubstantial Trinity, Father, Son, and Holy Ghost, now and ever, and to all eternity.

(Aloud.)

For unto thee is becoming and is due praise from us all, and honor, and adoration, and thanksgiving, Father, Son, and Holy Spirit, now and ever.

The Deacon.

In the peace of Christ let us sing:

And again he says:

In the peace of Christ let us go on:

The People.

In the name of the Lord. Sir, pronounce the blessing.

Dismission prayer, spoken by the Deacon.

Going on from glory to glory, we praise thee, the Saviour of our souls. Glory to Father, and Son, and Holy Spirit now and ever, and to all eternity. We praise thee, the Saviour of our souls.

The Priest says a prayer from the altar to the sacristy.

Going on from strength to strength, and having fulfilled all the divine service in thy temple, even now we beseech thee, O Lord our God, make us worthy of perfect loving kindness; make straight our path: root us in thy fear, and make us worthy of the heavenly kingdom, in Christ Jesus our Lord, with whom thou art blessed, together with thy all-holy, and good, and quickening Spirit, now and always, and forever.

The Deacon.

Again and again, and at all times, in peace let us beseech the Lord.

Prayer said in the sacristy after the dismissal.

Thou hast given unto us, O Lord, sanctification in the communion of the all-holy body and precious blood of thy only-begotten Son, our Lord Jesus Christ; give unto us also the grace of thy good Spirit, and keep us blameless in the faith, lead us unto perfect adoption and redemption, and to the coming joys of eternity; for thou art our sanctification and light, O God, and thy only-begotten Son, and thy all-holy Spirit, now and ever, and to all eternity. Amen.

The Deacon.

In the peace of Christ let us keep watch.

The Priest.

Blessed is God, who blesseth and sanctifieth through the communion of the holy, and quickening, and pure mysteries, now and ever, and to all eternity. Amen.

Then the prayer of propitiation.

O Lord Jesus Christ, Son of the living God, Lamb and Shepherd, who takest away the sin of the world, who didst freely forgive their debts to the two debtors, and gavest remission of her sins to the woman that was a sinner, who gavest healing to the paralytic, with the remission of his sins; forgive, remit, pardon, O God, our offenses, voluntary and involuntary, in knowledge and in ignorance, by transgression and by disobedience, which thy all-holy Spirit knows better than thy servants do:

And if men, carnal and dwelling in this world, have in aught erred from thy commandments, either moved by the devil, whether in word or in deed, or if they have come under a curse, or by reason of some special vow, I entreat and beseech thy unspeakable loving kindness, that they may be set free from their word, and released from the oath and the special vow, according to thy goodness.

Verily, O Sovereign Lord, hear my supplication on behalf of thy servants, and do thou pass by all their errors, remembering them no more; forgive them every transgression, voluntary and involuntary; deliver them from everlasting punishment: for thou art he that hast commanded us, saying, Whatsoever things ye bind upon earth, shall be bound in Heaven; and whatsoever things ye loose upon earth, shall be loosed in Heaven: for thou art our God, a God able to pity, and to save and to forgive sins; and glory is due unto thee, with the eternal Father, and the quickening Spirit, now and ever, and to all eternity. Amen.

THE DIVINE LITURGY OF SAINT JAMES

O God of love, who hast given a new commandment through thine only-begotten Son, that we should love one another, even as thou didst love us, the unworthy and the wandering, and gavest thy beloved Son for our life and salvation; we pray thee, Lord, give to us, thy servants, in all time of our life on the earth, a mind forgetful of past ill-will, a pure conscience and sincere thoughts, and a heart to love our brethren; for the sake of Jesus Christ, thy Son, our Lord and only Saviour.

COPTIC LITURGY OF SAINT CYRIL

MASTER and Lord, God the Almighty, the Father of our Lord Jesus Christ, we pray and beseech thee to send the peace which is from Heaven into the hearts of all of us, and grant us also the peace of this world, through Jesus Christ our Lord. Amen.

COPTIC LITURGY OF SAINT MARK

WE yield thee thanks, we yield thee exceeding thanks, O Lord our God, us touching all things, and for all things, through all things, and in all things; for that thou hast sheltered us, succored us, kept us, and brought us to this hour. If we have at all sinned against thee, in thought or word or deed, do thou, O lover of men, vouchsafe to overlook it; and forsake not us, O God, who put our trust in thee, nor lead us into temptation; but deliver us from the evil one, and from his works, through Jesus Christ our Lord. Amen.

COPTIC LITURGY OF SAINT MARK

WE pray and beseech thee, O good God, Lover of men, remember thy Church which is from one end of the earth to the other end thereof; bless all peoples and all lands. O King of peace, grant unto us thy peace, for thou hast given us all things. Possess us, O God, for beside thee we know none other. We are called by thy name; quicken our souls, for thou art our God. It is thou that loosest them that are bound, and raisest up them that are cast down. Thou art the Hope of the hopeless, the Help of the helpless, the Comfort of the weakhearted, the Harbor of the tempest-tossed. To every soul that is in affliction, and is oppressed, give rest, refreshment, and help. O Physician of souls and bodies, Overseer of all flesh, visit us with thy salvation, through Jesus Christ our Lord. Amen.

COPTIC LITURGY OF SAINT MARK

WE pray and beseech thee, O good God and Lover of men, to send down the very Paraclete, the Spirit of truth, holy and life-giving, who spake in the Law and by the prophets and apostles, who is everywhere present, who fillest all things, and workest by his own free will. And this we pray, through Jesus Christ our Lord. Amen.

COPTIC LITURGY OF SAINT MARK

O Lord of knowledge, and Dispenser of wisdom, who discoverest deep things out of darkness, O Lover of men, bestow on us a mind without distraction, and a purified understanding, that we may know how profitable are thy holy teachings, through Jesus Christ our Lord. Amen.

COPTIC LITURGY OF SAINT MARK

IT is meet and right, it is expedient for our souls and bodies, eternal Master, Lord God the Father Almighty, at all times and in all places, to praise thee, to hymn thee, to bless thee, to serve thee, to adore thee, to give thanks to thee, to glorify thee, to confess to thee, with unsilenced heart and unwearied doxologies. Thou art he who hast made the heavens and the things that are in the heavens, the earth and all things that are therein. Thou art he who hast made man after thine own image, and made all things through thy wisdom. For these things we give thanks from the rising of the sun unto the going down of the same, and from the north to the south, through Jesus Christ our Lord. Amen.

COPTIC LITURGY OF SAINT MARK

WE pray and beseech thee of thy goodness, O Lover of men, grant us thy mercy, and loose the bonds of our sins. If we have done aught amiss, wittingly or unwittingly—whether in word, or in deed, or from faintheartedness—do thou, who knowest the feebleness of men, as a good God bestow on us the forgiveness of our sins. Bless us, purify us, absolve us, and direct us into thy holy will; for thou art our God, through Jesus Christ our Lord. Amen.

COPTIC LITURGY OF SAINT MARK

O Lord, O Lord, it is not meet that thou shouldest come beneath the roof of my polluted house, for I have provoked thee to anger and moved thee to wrath and have done evil in thy sight and have polluted my soul and body, and in me there is not one good deed. But because thou wast made and didst become man for my salvation, for the sake of thy precious cross and thy life-giving death and thy resurrection on the third day, I pray thee and entreat thee to purify me from all transgression and curse and sin; and when I receive the mystery of thy holy things be it not unto me for a reproach or for condemnation, but have mercy on me and pity me in the multitude of thy mercy, and grant me pardon for my sin and life for my soul, through the prayer of our Lady Mary and John the Baptist and for the sake of all the saints and martyrs for ever and ever.

ETHIOPIC ANAPHORA OF THE APOSTLES

THE Lord bless us his servants in peace. Be it unto us for forgiveness that we have received thy body and blood. Suffer us by the Spirit to tread on all the power of the enemy. The blessing of thy holy hand which is full of mercy, it we all hope for. Remove from us every work of evil; unite us to every work of good. Blessed be he who hath given us his holy body and precious blood. Grace have we received and life have we found by the power of the cross of Jesus Christ. To thee, O Lord, we give thanks, having received the grace which is from the Holy Spirit.

ETHIOPIC ANAPHORA OF THE APOSTLES

REMEMBER, O Lord, those who have asked remembrances in our prayers. Give rest to them that have fallen asleep before us, and heal them that are sick; for thou art the Life, and the Hope, and the Raiser up of us all; that so to thee we may send up thanksgiving into highest Heaven, world without end, through Jesus Christ our Lord. Amen.

LITURGY OF THE ARMENIAN JACOBITES

MINGLE, O Lord, our humanity with thy divinity, thy greatness with our humility, and our humility with thy greatness, through Jesus Christ our Lord. Amen.

LITURGY OF SAINT GREGORY OF ARMENIA

O Lord our God, save thy people and bless thine inheritance, guard the fullness of thy Church; sanctify those who in love come to greet the beauty of thy house; glorify us, O Lord, by thy divine power, and forsake not those who put their trust in thee; for thine is the power, and the dominion, and the glory, world without end, through Jesus Christ our Lord. Amen.

LITURGY OF THE ARMENIANS

ELEVEN

Prayers from Greek Liturgies

NO one who is bound by earthly desires and lusts is worthy to come near to thee, to approach thee, to minister to thee, O King of glory: for to serve thee is a thing great and terrible, even to the heavenly powers. Yet through thy unspeakable and immeasurable love of men, thou who without change or loss didst become man, and didst take the title of our High Priest, hast given us the ministry of this liturgic and unbloody sacrifice, being thyself Lord of all things. For thou only, O Lord our God, dost reign in Heaven and on earth, who sittest upon the throne of the cherubim, Lord of the seraphim, King of Israel, who only art holy, and restest among the holy. I therefore pray thee, thou the only gracious and merciful Lord, look down upon me a sinner, and thine unprofitable servant, cleanse my soul and my heart from an evil conscience; and by the power of thy Holy Spirit, grant me, whom thou hast endued with the grace of the priesthood, to stand before this thy holy table, and to consecrate thy sacred and spotless body and precious blood. For to thee I approach, with bowed neck, and beseech thee to turn not thy face away from me, nor reject me from among thy children, but rather deign that these gifts be offered by me a sinner, thy unworthy servant. For thou thyself dost offer and art offered, dost receive and art received, Christ our God. And to thee we give praise together with thine eternal Father and thine all-holy, good and life-giving Spirit, now and forever, eternally. Amen.

PREPARATION PRAYER OF SAINT JOHN CHRYSOSTOM

THE grace of our Lord Jesus Christ, and the love of God the Father, and the fellowship of the Holy Ghost, be with you all.

And with thy spirit.

Let us lift up our hearts.

We lift them up unto the Lord.

Let us give thanks unto the Lord.

It is meet and right to worship Father, Son, and Holy Ghost, the consubstantial and undivided Trinity.

O Sovereign Lord, God the Father, who art almighty and adorable; it is indeed very meet, right, and agreeable to the majesty of thy holiness, that we should sing praises to thee, bless thee, worship thee, give thanks to thee, glorify thee, the only true God; and with a contrite heart and humble spirit offer to thee this our reasonable service. For it is thou who hast called us to the knowledge of thy truth. But who is able to talk of thy power, to shew forth thy praise, and tell of all thy wondrous works? O thou governor of all things, Lord of Heaven and earth, and of every creature, whether visible or invisible, who sittest upon the throne of glory, and from thence beholdest the vast abyss, self-existing, invisible, incomprehensible, and immutable; the Father of our Lord Jesus Christ, the great God and Saviour of our hope; who is the express image of thy goodness, and the lively representation of thee his Father; the living word, God before all ages, wisdom, life, holiness, power, the true light whence proceeded the Holy Spirit, the spirit of truth, the grace of adoption, and pledge of our future inheritance, the first fruits of eternal good things, the life-giving power, and the fountain of holiness, by whom all reasonable and intelligent creatures are empowered to serve and praise thee: for all things do serve thee, angels, archangels, thrones, dominions, principalities, authorities, powers, the many eyed cherubim, and seraphim, with six wings, who with twain cover their faces, and with twain their feet, and with twain they fly, crying one to another incessantly, and with uninterrupted praises, singing, shouting, crying aloud, and saying the triumphal hymn.

Holy, holy, holy, Lord of Sabaoth, Heaven and earth are full of thy glory, hosanna in the highest; blessed is he that cometh in the name of the Lord, hosanna in the highest.

With those blessed powers, O merciful Lord, we, unworthy sinners, cry aloud, and say; thou art indeed truly holy, thy holiness is perfect, infinite, manifesting itself in all thy works; for in righteousness and true judgment hast thou done all things. When thou hadst formed man out of the dust of the earth, and honored him, O God, with thine own image impressed upon him; thou didst place him in a paradise of pleasure, with a promise of rewarding his obedience to thy commands with immortality and eternal happiness. But when, overreached by the subtilty of the serpent, he became disobedient to thee, and by his transgressions was made subject to death; thou, O God, in thy just judgment, didst drive him out of paradise, and reduce him again to earth whence he was taken, preparing for him however a new birth to everlasting life, which is in thy Christ. For thou wast not always wroth with thy creature, or for ever unmindful of the work of thine own hands, but in thine abundant pity didst in divers manners visit him with a providential care. Thou didst send thy prophets, and shew mighty works through thy saints, who pleased thee in all ages. Thou spakest to us by the mouth of thy servants the prophets, who foretold us of a salvation to come. Thou appointedst the law for our direction, and guardian angels for our preservation. And when the fullness of time was come, thou spakest unto us by thy Son, by whom thou hadst made the worlds. Who being the brightness of thy glory, and the express image of thy person, upholding all things by the word of his power, thought it no robbery to be equal to thee his God and Father. Nevertheless he who was God from all eternity, came down from Heaven, conversed with mankind, was incarnate of the Virgin Mary, debased himself to the form of a servant, making himself in his humiliation like unto us, that he might raise us to the likeness of the image of his glory. For as by man sin entered into the world, and death by sin; it seemed good to thine only-begotten Son, who is in the bosom of thee his God and Father, being made of a woman, the holy Mother of God, and ever Virgin Mary, and under the law to triumph over sin in his own flesh, that those who died in Adam, might be made alive in him, thy Christ. He conversed in the world, instructed us in the way of salvation, brought us from our idolatry, to the knowledge of thee our true God and Father, purchasing us to himself for a peculiar people, a royal priesthood, an holy nation; and having baptized us with water for the remission of our sins, and sanctified us with the Holy Ghost, he gave himself a ransom to redeem us from death, by which we were detained, being by our sins become his prey; and descending through the cross into Hell, that he might fulfill all things in himself, he loosed the pains of death; and rising again the third day, he led the way to a resurrection of all flesh from the dead, forasmuch as it was impossible for the author of life to be held of corruption: He became the first fruits of them that slept, and the first-begotten from the dead, that he might be the first of all in all things. And ascending up into Heaven, he sat down at the right hand of thy majesty on high, who shall likewise come again to render to every man according to his works. But he has left to us a memorial of his saving passion, these gifts which we have now offered according to his command: for when he was just going out to his voluntary, glorious, and life-giving death, in the same night wherein he gave up himself for the life of the world, taking bread into his holy and immaculate hands, and presenting it to thee his God and Father, he gave thanks, blessed, sanctified, and brake it.

He gave it to his holy disciples and apostles, saying, Take, eat; this is my body, which is broken for you for the remission of sins.

Amen.

In like manner taking, mixing, giving thanks, blessing, sanctifying the cup of the fruit of the vine.

He gave it to his holy disciples and apostles, saying, Drink ye all of this; this is my blood of the New Testament, which is shed for you, and for many, for the remission of sins.

Amen.

Do this in remembrance of me: for as oft as ye eat this bread, and drink this cup, ye shew forth my death, and confess my resurrection. Wherefore we also, O Lord, having in remembrance those things which he suffered for our salvation, his life-giving cross, his lying in the grave for three days, his resurrection from the dead, his ascension into Heaven, his session at the right hand of thee his God and Father, and his glorious and terrible second appearance, through all, and in all, offer to thee thine own, out of thine own gifts.

We praise thee, we bless thee, we give thanks to thee, O Lord, and make our supplications to thee, O our God.

Wherefore, O most holy Lord, we sinners, thy unworthy servants, to whom thou hast vouchsafed the honor to minister unto thee; not upon account of our own righteousness (for we have done nothing praise-worthy) but according to thy mercies and compassions which thou hast liberally bestowed upon us, approach thy holy altar: and laying before thee these symbols of the holy body and blood of thy Christ, we pray and beseech thee, O thou holy of holies, of thy gracious goodness to send down thine Holy Spirit upon us, and upon these gifts, to bless, to sanctify, and to perfect them. Amen.

THE ANAPHORA OF SAINT BASIL

WE offer to thee this reasonable and unbloody worship, and beg, pray, beseech thee to send down thine Holy Spirit upon us and upon these gifts lying before thee.

Make this bread the precious body of thy Christ and what is in this cup, the precious blood of thy Christ, changing them by thy Holy Spirit, so that it may be to those who partake of it for sobriety, the remission of sins, the communication of the Holy Ghost, the fullness of the kingdom of heaven; for confidence in thee and not for judgment or condemnation.

We offer, moreover, this reasonable worship for those who are departed from us in faith, our forefathers, fathers, patriarchs, prophets, apostles, preachers, evangelists, martyrs, confessors, chaste persons, and every spirit perfected in faith, especially the most holy, immaculate, blessed above all, most glorious lady, the mother of God, and ever-virgin Mary.

Saint John the prophet, the forerunner of our Saviour and the Baptist; the holy and renowned apostles, whom we commemorate, and all other thy saints: for the sake of whose prayers, O God, look upon us; and be mindful of those who rest in hope of a resurrection to eternal life.

For the rest and forgiveness of the soul of thy servant:

Give it rest, O God, in a pleasant place where there is no sorrow or mourning but where it may rejoice in the light of thy countenance. We beseech thee likewise, O Lord, to remember all orthodox bishops and those who rightly divide the Word of Truth, the presbyters and deacons in Christ, and all others of the ministerial order. We offer likewise this reasonable worship for the whole world; for the holy catholic and apostolic Church; for all who lead their lives in chastity and holiness; for our emperors who live in the faith and love of Christ, for their court and camp. Give them, O Lord, a peaceable reign, that in their peace we also may lead a quiet and peaceable life in all godliness and honesty.

Remember, O Lord, our most sacred Metropolitan.

Remember, O Lord, this city wherein we dwell, and every other city and country, and all the faithful who dwell in them. Remember, O Lord, all that travel by land or by water, all that labor under sickness or salvery; remember them for health and safety. Remember, O Lord, those in thy holy Church who bring forth good works, and forget not the poor. Grant unto us all thy mercy and loving kindness.

And grant that we may with one mouth, and one heart, praise and glorify thy great and glorious name, Father, Son, and Holy Ghost, now, henceforth, and forever.

LITURGY OF SAINT JOHN CHRYSOSTOM

ALMIGHTY God, who hast given us grace at this time with one accord to make our common supplications unto thee; and dost promise, that when two or three are gathered together in thy name thou wilt grant their requests: Fulfill now, O Lord, the desires and petitions of thy servants, as may be most expedient for them; granting us in this world knowledge of thy truth, and in the world to come life everlasting.

SAINT JOHN CHRYSOSTOM

T W E L V E

Prayers from Latin Liturgies

PRIEST: Brethren, pray that my sacrifice and yours may be acceptable to God the Father Almighty.

May the Lord receive the sacrifice from thy hands, to the praise and glory of his name, to our benefit, and to that of all his holy Church.

The Lord be with you.

And with thy Spirit.

Lift up your hearts.

We lift them up unto the Lord.

Let us give thanks unto our Lord God.

It is meet and right so to do.

It is very meet, right, and our bounden duty, that we should at all times and in all places, give thanks unto thee, O Lord, Holy Father, Almighty, Everlasting God. Through Christ our Lord: by whom the angels laud, the dominations adore, the powers do hold in awe thy majesty, the Heavens and the heavenly virtues, together with the blessed seraphim, in exultation celebrate thy praise. With whom, we pray thee, let us join our voices, humbly saying:

Holy, holy, holy, Lord God of hosts, Heaven and earth are full of thy glory; glory be to thee, O Lord most high.

Blessed is he that cometh in the name of the Lord. Hosanna in the highest.

Therefore, O most merciful Father, we humbly pray and beseech thee, through Jesus Christ thy Son, our Lord, to accept and to bless these gifts, these offerings, these holy, unspotted sacrifices, which we offer unto thee, firstly, for thy holy catholic Church, which may it please thee to keep in peace, to preserve, unite, and govern throughout all the world, and also for thy servant, N, our Pope, N, our Bishop, and for all orthodox believers and professors of the catholic and apostolic faith.

Be mindful, O Lord, of thy servants and handmaidens, N and N.

And of all here present, whose faith thou knowest, and whose devotion thou beholdest; for whom we do offer, or who do themselves offer unto thee this sacrifice of praise for themselves, for all their kinfolk, for the redemption of their souls, for the hope of their safety and salvation, and do pay their vows unto thee, the eternal God, the living and the true.

Joining in communion with, and reverencing the memory, firstly of the glorious and ever-virgin Mary, Mother of our God and Lord Jesus Christ; and also of the blessed apostles and martyrs, Peter and Paul, Andrew, James, John, Thomas, James, Philip, Bartholomew, Matthew, Simon and Thaddeus; Linus, Cletus, Clement, Sixtus, Cornelius, Cyprian, Laurence, Chrysogonus, John and Paul, Cosmas and Damian, and of all thy saints; by whose merits and prayers do thou grant that in all things we may be defended by the help of thy protection. Through the same Christ our Lord. Amen.

This oblation, therefore, of our service, and also of thy whole family, we beseech thee, O Lord, graciously to accept; and do thou order our days in thy peace, deliver us from eternal damnation, and suffer us to be numbered in the flock of thine elect. Through Christ our Lord. Amen.

Which oblation do thou, O God, vouchsafe in all things to make blessed, approved, ratified, reasonable, and acceptable, that it may become to us the body and blood of thy most dearly beloved Son, Jesus Christ our Lord.

Who the day before he suffered took bread into his holy and venerable hands, and lifting his eyes to Heaven, to thee, O God, his Father Almighty, when he had given thanks he blessed it and brake it and gave it to his disciples, saying, Take, eat ye all of this; for this is my body.

Likewise after supper he took this glorious cup into his holy and venerable hands, and when he had given thanks to thee he blessed it and gave it to his disciples, saying, Take and drink ye all of this; for this is the cup of the new and eternal testament in my blood; the mystery of faith; which is shed for you and for many for the remission of sins. As often as ye shall do this ye shall do it in remembrance of me.

Wherefore, O Lord, we thy servants, and thy holy people, mindful of the ever-blessed passion of the same Christ thy Son our Lord, his resurrection from the dead, and glorious ascension into Heaven, do offer unto thy most glorious majesty, of thine own bounteous gifts, a pure offering, a holy offering, a spotless offering, even the holy bread of eternal life, and the cup of everlasting salvation.

Upon which vouchsafe to look with a favorable and gracious countenance, and to accept them, even as it pleased thee to accept the gifts of thy righteous servant Abel, and the sacrifice of our patriarch Abraham, and the holy sacrifice, the spotless offering which thy high priest Melchisedech offered unto thee.

We humbly beseech thee, almighty God, to command that these be carried by the hands of thy holy angel to thy altar on high, in the sight of thy divine majesty, that as many of us as by participation at this altar shall receive the most sacred body and blood of thy Son may be filled with all heavenly benediction and grace. Through the same Christ our Lord. Amen.

Be mindful also, O Lord, of thy servants and handmaidens, N. and N., who are gone hence before us with the sign of faith, and do now rest in the sleep of peace. To them, O Lord, and to all that rest in Christ, grant, we beseech thee, a place of refreshment, of light, and of peace. Through Christ our Lord.

And to us, also, thy sinful servants, trusting in the multitude of thy mercies, vouchsafe to grant some part and fellowship with thy holy apostles and martyrs; with John, Stephen, Matthias, Barnabas, Ignatius, Alexander, Marcellinus, Peter, Felicity, Perpetua, Agatha, Lucy, Agnes, Cicely, Anastasia, and with all thy saints: into whose company we beseech thee to admit us, not weighing our merits, but pardoning our offenses. Through Christ our Lord.

By whom, O Lord, thou dost ever create, sanctify, quicken, bless, and bestow upon us all these good things.

Through whom and with whom and in whom, be unto thee, O God, the Father Almighty, in the unity of the Holy Ghost, all honor and glory, world without end. Amen.

OLD ROMAN CANON

HEAR us, Lord, and have mercy.

With every confidence we call on the Father of the Only-begotten, the Son of the eternal Father and our Lord the Holy Spirit.

Kyrie eleison.

For the spotless Church of the living God, everywhere throughout the world, we appeal to the God who is rich in goodness.

Kyrie eleison.

For the great God's holy priests, the ministers at the sacred altar, and all the peoples that worship the true God, we offer our prayers to Christ the Lord.

Kyrie eleison.

For those who preach the true word as they ought, we pray with special earnestness to God's Word in his infinite wisdom.

Kyrie eleison.

For all who, keeping themselves chaste in soul and body to obtain the kingdom of Heaven, spend themselves in those labors that befit the spiritual, we implore the Giver of spiritual gifts.

Kyrie eleison.

For Christian princes and their armies, loving justice and equity, we beseech the omnipotent God.

Kyrie eleison.

For mild and pleasant weather, for rain at the time it is needed, for healthy and gentle winds and for the seasons to follow one another to our advantage, we entreat the Ruler of the universe.

Kyrie eleison.

To those who have acquired some knowledge of Christianity and some desire for its heavenly grace, we beg the all-powerful God to show his mercy.

Kyrie eleison.

For those beset by the frailty inherent in this weak human nature, by the envy of evil spirits or by any of the world's errors, we ask our Redeemer's mercy.

Kyrie eleison.

For those who are forced to live abroad, those persecuted by men who wield their power unjustly, and those harassed by enemy action, we implore our Lord and Saviour.

Kyrie eleison.

For those deceived by the false teaching of the Jews . . . or the heretics' crooked reasoning and for those sunk in pagan superstition, we make our prayer to the God of truth.

Kyrie eleison.

To those whose religion moves them to labor for him, and to those who out of love for their brethren relieve the wants of the needy, we pray the Lord to show his great mercy.

Kyrie eleison.

For all who ever cross the threshold of this holy house . . . and for those assembled here now from motives of religion and humble devotion, we offer our prayers to the Lord in his glory.

Kyrie eleison.

For the cleansing of our bodies and souls and the forgiveness of all our sins, we entreat the God of boundless compassion.

Kyrie eleison.

For rest for the souls of all the faithful, especially those of the Lord's holy priests who have governed this Catholic Church, we pray the Lord of the spirits and Judge of all flesh.

Kyrie eleison.

Bodies dead to sin and souls alive by faith,
grant us, Lord, grant us.
Holy fear and true love,
grant us, Lord, grant us.
Lives that please you, deaths you can approve of,
grant us, Lord, grant us.

Angels to bring us peace and saints to assist us,
grant us, Lord, grant us.
Ourselves and all that we have we owe to the Lord. He gave them, he increased them, he gives us the means to keep them. To his mercy we commend them, and to the judgment of his providence.
Lord, have mercy.

ROMAN LITANY

ALMIGHTY God, who shewest to them that be in error the light of thy truth, to the intent that they may return into the way of righteousness, grant unto all them that are admitted into the fellowship of Christ's religion, that they may eschew those things that are contrary to their profession, and follow all such things as are agreeable to the same, through Jesus Christ our Lord.

Almighty and merciful God, of whose only gift it cometh that thy faithful people do unto thee true and laudable service; grant, we beseech thee, that we may so faithfully serve thee in this life, that we fail not finally to attain thy heavenly promises, through Jesus Christ our Lord.

Grant to us, Lord, we beseech thee, the spirit to think and do always such things as be rightful: that we, who cannot do anything that is good without thee, may by thee be enabled to live according to thy will, through Jesus Christ our Lord.

Grant, O Lord, we beseech thee, that the course of this world may be so peaceably ordered by thy governance, that thy Church may joyfully serve thee in all godly quietness, through Jesus Christ our Lord.

Let thy merciful ears, O Lord, be open to the prayers of thy humble servants; and that they may obtain their petitions make them to ask such things as shall please thee, through Jesus Christ our Lord.

LEONINE SACRAMENTARY

MERCIFULLY regard, O Lord, the prayers of thy family, and while they submit themselves to thee with their whole heart, do thou prosper, support, encompass them; that relying on thee as their guide, they may be entangled in no evils, and replenished with all good; through Jesus Christ our Lord.

We beseech Thee, O Lord, in thy loving kindness, set in order our life and conversation, that no adversities may prevail against us, and nothing salutary be wanting to us, through Jesus Christ our Lord.

LEONINE SACRAMENTARY

IN thy mercy and majesty, O Lord, behold thy household, that they may be neither stained with vices of their own, nor held in bondage by the sins of others; but that being ever freed and cleansed from both, they may do service unto thee; through Jesus Christ our Lord.

Hear us, O Lord, our God, and separate the hearts of thy faithful people from the wickedness of the world; that they who call thee Lord with their own voice may not fall back into the service of the Devil; through Jesus Christ our Lord.

Grant, we beseech thee, Almighty God, that pressing onward in thy way with devout minds, we may escape the snares of the sins that beset us; through Jesus Christ our Lord.

LEONINE SACRAMENTARY

LET thy perpetual mercy, O Lord, accompany thy Church; that while it is placed among the storms of the world, it may both be refreshed with present gladness, and behold the brightness of eternal bliss; through Jesus Christ our Lord.

Grant us, we beseech thee, O Lord our God, ever to rejoice in devotion to thee; because our happiness is perpetual and full, if we are continually serving the author of all good; through Jesus Christ our Lord.

We beseech thee, O Lord, let thy faithful people rejoice evermore in thy benefits; that being ordered by thy governance, they may please thee in their lives, and happily obtain the good which they pray for; through Jesus Christ our Lord.

Grant, O almighty God, that we may attain to the fullness of joy, and be the more earnestly devoted to thy majesty; through Jesus Christ our Lord.

LEONINE SACRAMENTARY

GRANT, O merciful God, that he who was born this day to be the Saviour of the world, as he is the author of our divine birth, so may be himself the bestower of our immortality; through the same Jesus Christ our Lord.

Almighty and everlasting God, who hast willed that on the nativity of our Lord Jesus Christ, thy Son, should depend the beginning and the completion of all religion; grant us, we beseech thee, to be reckoned as a portion of him, on whom is built the whole salvation of mankind.

We beseech thee, O Lord, bestow on thy servants the increase of faith, hope, and charity; that as they glory in the nativity of thy Son our Lord, they may, by thy governance, not feel the adversities of this world; and also that what they desire to celebrate in time, they may enjoy to all eternity; through the same Jesus Christ our Lord.

O God, who art pleased to save, by the nativity of thy Christ, the race of man, which was mortally wounded in its chief; grant, we beseech thee, that we may not cleave to the author of our perdition, but be transferred to the fellowship of our redeemer.

Grant unto us, we pray thee, O Lord our God, that we who rejoice to keep the feast of the nativity of Jesus Christ our Lord, may by walking worthily of him attain to fellowship with him, through the same Jesus Christ our Lord.

Grant, O Lord, we beseech thee, to thy people an inviolable firmness of faith; that as they confess thine only-begotten Son, the everlasting partaker of thy glory, to have been born in our very flesh, of the Virgin Mother, they may be delivered from present adversities, and admitted into joys that shall abide; through the same Jesus Christ our Lord.

Grant, we beseech thee, O Lord, our God, that thy Church may alike apprehend both parts of the one mystery, and adore one Christ.

O God, who dividest the day from the night, separate our deeds from the gloom of darkness, that ever meditating on things holy, we may continually live in thy light; through Jesus Christ our Lord.

LEONINE SACRAMENTARY

ALMIGHTY and everlasting God, who restorest us by the blessed passion of thy Christ, preserve in us the works of thy mercy; that by the celebration of this mystery our lives may be continually devout; through the same Jesus Christ our Lord.

We beseech thee, O Lord, purify thy family, and cleanse it from all contagion of wickedness; that the vessels which have been redeemed by their Lord's passion may never again be stained by the unclean spirit, but may be possessed by everlasting salvation; through the same Jesus Christ our Lord.

LEONINE SACRAMENTARY

BE present, O Lord, to our supplications; that as we trust that the Saviour of mankind is seated with thee in thy majesty, so we may feel that, according to his promise, he abideth with us unto the end of the world; through the same Jesus Christ our Lord.

Almighty and everlasting God, vouchsafe unto us, by the gift of this day's festival, that the aims of thy children may thither be directed, where our substance, in thine only-begotten Son, is with thee; through the same Jesus Christ our Lord.

Hear us, O merciful God, and grant our minds to be lifted up, whither our redeemer hath ascended; that at the second coming of the mediator we may receive from thy manifested bounty what we now venture to hope for as a promised gift; through the same Jesus Christ our Lord.

Grant, we beseech thee, Almighty God, that the faithful members of thy Son may thither follow, whither our head and chief has gone before.

LEONINE SACRAMENTARY

WE beseech thee, O Lord, let the strong crying of thy Church ascend to the ears of thy loving kindness; that receiving forgiveness of sins, it may become devout by the working of thy grace, and tranquil under the protection of thy power; through Jesus Christ our Lord.

Look mercifully, O good shepherd, on thy flock; and suffer not the sheep which thou hast redeemed with precious blood to be torn in pieces by the assaults of the Devil.

O God, who hast promised that thou wilt never be absent from thy church unto the end of the world, and that the gates of Hell shall never prevail against the apostolic confession; graciously make thy strength perfect in our weakness, and show the efficacy of thy divine promise, while thou deignest even to be present in thy feeble ones. For then do we beyond doubt feel thy presence, when thou dispensest to each one, at all times, in fitting manner, things desirable, and by perpetual protection guardest us from the attack of all our adversaries.

LEONINE SACRAMENTARY

O Lord our God, refresh us with quiet sleep, when we are wearied with the day's labor; that being assisted with the help which our weakness needs, we may be devoted to thee both in body and mind; through Jesus Christ our Lord.

Be present, O Lord, to our prayers, and protect us by day and night; that in all successive changes of times we may ever be strengthened by thine unchangeableness; through Jesus Christ our Lord.

LEONINE SACRAMENTARY

ALMIGHTY and everlasting God, by whose spirit the whole body of the Church is governed and sanctified, receive our supplications and prayers, which we offer before thee for all estates of men in thy holy Church; that every member of the same, in his vocation and ministry, may truly and godly serve thee, through Jesus Christ our Lord.

O God, the strength of all them that put their trust in thee, mercifully accept our prayers; and because through the weakness of our mortal nature we can do no good thing without thee, grant us the help of thy grace; that in keeping of thy commandments we may please thee, both in will and deed, through Jesus Christ our Lord.

O God, forasmuch as without thee we are not able to please thee, mercifully grant, that thy Holy Spirit may in all things direct and rule our hearts, through Jesus Christ our Lord.

O God, from whom all holy desires, all good counsels, and all just works do proceed; give unto thy servants that peace which the world cannot give; that both our hearts may be set to obey thy commandments, and also that by thee we being defended from the fear of our enemies may pass our time in rest and quietness, through Jesus Christ our Lord.

O God, who declarest thy almighty power most chiefly in shewing mercy and pity; mercifully grant unto us such a measure of thy grace, that we, running the way of thy commandments, may obtain thy gracious promises, and be made partakers of thy heavenly treasure, through Jesus Christ our Lord.

O God, who hast prepared for them that love thee such good things as pass man's understanding, pour into our hearts such love toward thee, that we, loving thee above all things, may obtain thy promises, which exceed all that we can desire, through Jesus Christ our Lord.

O God, who art the author of peace and lover of concord, in knowledge of whom standeth our eternal life, whose service is perfect freedom, defend us thy humble servants in all assaults of our enemies; that we, surely trusting in thy defense, may not fear the power of any adversaries, through Jesus Christ our Lord.

O almighty and most merciful God, of thy bountiful goodness keep us, we beseech thee, from all things that may hurt us; that we, being ready both in body and soul, may cheerfully accomplish those things that thou wouldest have done, through Jesus Christ our Lord.

Almighty and everlasting God, who art always more ready to hear than we to pray, and art wont to give more than either we desire, or deserve, pour down upon us the abundance of thy mercy; forgiving us those things whereof our conscience is afraid, and giving us those good things which we are not worthy to ask, through Jesus Christ our Lord.

GELASIAN SACRAMENTARY

O Lord, who never failest to help and govern them whom thou dost bring up in thy steadfast fear and love; keep us, we beseech thee, under the protection of thy good providence, and make us to have a perpetual fear and love of thy holy name, through Jesus Christ our Lord.

Lighten our darkness, we beseech thee, O Lord, and by thy great mercy defend us from all perils and dangers of this night, for the love of thy only Son, our Saviour, Jesus Christ.

Grant, we beseech thee, merciful Lord, to thy faithful people, pardon and peace, that they may be cleansed from all their sins, and serve thee with a quiet mind, through Jesus Christ our Lord.

Keep, we beseech thee, O Lord, thy Church with thy

perpetual mercy; and, because the frailty of man without thee cannot but fall, keep us ever by thy help from all things hurtful; and lead us to all things profitable to our salvation, through Jesus Christ our Lord.

Assist us mercifully, O Lord, in these our supplications and prayers, and dispose the way of thy servants toward the attainment of everlasting salvation; that, among all the changes and chances of this mortal life, they may ever be defended by thy most gracious and ready help, through Jesus Christ our Lord.

Lord, we beseech thee, grant thy people grace to withstand the temptations of the world, the flesh, and the Devil, and with pure hearts and minds to follow thee the only God, through Jesus Christ our Lord.

Lord of all power and might, who art the author and giver of all good things, graft in our hearts the love of thy name, increase in us true religion, nourish us with all goodness, and of thy great mercy keep us in the same, through Jesus Christ our Lord.

O Lord, from whom all good things do come, grant to us thy humble servants, that by thy holy inspiration we may think those things that be good, and by thy merciful guiding may perform the same, through Jesus Christ our Lord.

GELASIAN SACRAMENTARY

V. The Prayers of Saint Augustine

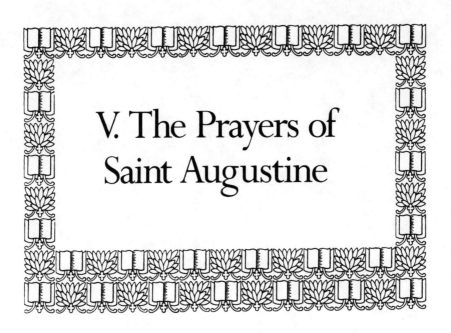

THE prayers of Saint Augustine, Bishop of Hippo (354–430), represent the largest and most theologically nuanced body of devotional writings to survive from the early Church. Influenced by Saint Ambrose, he extended the theological and existential range of personal prayer, combining the specifically Christian themes of fall and redemption, the keen insights of a logician, and the rich imagery of an accomplished rhetorician. Even as early Christian theology reaches its apogee with Saint Augustine, his prayers, as profound as they are accessible, represent the height of early Christian devotional literature.

We include here a selection of Augustine's prayers from three different sources; his autobigraphical *Confessions* (a book that has led some scholars to describe Augustine as the first "modern" man), his sermons and theological tracts, and his *Soliloquies*.

The *Confessions* are Augustine's tale of his own struggle for faith and his developing relationship with God. Written in an intensely personal style, his prayers are the archetype for many of our own.

Augustine's prayers from his more formal theological tractates, sermons, and commentaries demonstrate his deep commitment to others and to the life of the Church.

The long prayer from the *Soliloquies* is a personal credo in which Augustine incorporates the major themes of his theology.

THIRTEEN

Confessions

GREAT art thou, O Lord, and greatly to be praised; great is thy power, and thy wisdom infinite. And thee would man praise; man, but a particle of thy creation; man, that bears about him his mortality, the witness of his sin, the witness that thou resistest the proud: yet would man praise thee; he, but a particle of thy creation. Thou awakest us to delight in thy praise; for thou madest us for thyself, and our heart is restless, until it repose in thee. Grant me, Lord, to know and understand which is first, to call on thee or to praise thee? And, again, to know thee or to call on thee? For who can call on thee, not knowing thee? For he that knoweth thee not, may call on thee as other than thou art. Or, is it rather, that we call on thee that we may know thee? but how shall they call on him in whom they have not believed? Or how shall they believe without a preacher? And they that seek the Lord shall praise him: for they that seek shall find him, and they that find shall praise him. I will seek thee, Lord, by calling on thee; and will call on thee, believing in thee; for to us hast thou been preached. My faith, Lord, shall call on thee, which thou hast given me, wherewith thou hast inspired me, through the incarnation of thy Son, through the ministry of the Preacher.

And how shall I call upon my God, my God and Lord, since, when I call for him, I shall be calling him to myself? And what room is there within me, whither my God can come into me? Whither can God come into me, God who made Heaven and earth? Is there, indeed, O Lord my God, aught in me that can contain thee? Do then Heaven and earth, which thou hast made, and wherein thou hast made me, contain thee? Or, because nothing which exists could exist without thee, doth therefore whatever exists contain thee? Since, then, I too exist, why do I seek that thou shouldest enter into me, who were not, wert thou not in me? Why? Because I am not gone down in Hell, and yet thou art there also. For if I go down into Hell, thou art there. I could not be then, O my God, could not be at all, wert thou not in me; or rather, unless I were in thee, of whom are all things, by whom are all things, in whom are all things? Even so, Lord, even so. Whither do I call thee, since I am in thee? Or whence canst thou enter into me? for whither can I go beyond Heaven and earth, that thence my God should come into me, who hath said, I fill the Heaven and the earth.

Do the Heaven and earth then contain thee, since thou fillest them? Or dost thou fill them and yet overflow, since they do not contain thee? And whither, when the Heaven and the earth are filled, pourest thou forth the remainder of thyself? Or hast thou no need that aught contain thee, who containest all things, since what thou fillest thou fillest by containing it? For the vessels which thou fillest uphold thee not sincc, though they were broken. Thou wert not poured out. And when thou art poured out on us, thou art not cast down but thou upliftest us; thou art not dissipated, but thou gatherest us. But thou who fillest all things, fillest thou them with thy whole self? Or, since all things cannot contain thee wholly, do they contain part of thee? and all at once the same part? Or each its own part, the greater more, the smaller less? And is, then, one part of thee greater, another less? Or, art thou wholly everywhere, while nothing contains thee wholly?

What art thou then, my God? What, but the Lord

God? For who is Lord but the Lord? Or who is God save our God? Most highest, most good, most potent, most omnipotent; most merciful, yet most just; most hidden, yet most present; most beautiful, yet most strong; stable, yet incomprehensible; unchangeable, yet all-changing; never new, never old; all-renewing, and bringing age upon the proud, and they know it not; ever working, ever at rest; still gathering, yet nothing lacking; supporting, filling, and overspreading; creating, nourishing, and maturing; seeking, yet having all things. Thou lovest, without passion; art jealous, without anxiety; repentest, yet grievest not; art angry, yet serene; changest thy works, thy purpose unchanged; receivest again what thou findest, yet didst never lose; never in need, yet rejoicing in gains; never covetous, yet exacting usury. Thou receivest over and above, that thou mayest owe; and who hath aught that is not thine? Thou payest debts, owing nothing; remittest debts, losing nothing. And what had I now said, my God, my life, my holy joy? or what saith any man when he speaks of thee? Yet woe to him that speaketh not, since mute are even the most eloquent.

Oh! that I might repose on thee! Oh! that thou wouldest enter into my heart, and inebriate it, that I may forget my ills, and embrace thee, my sole good. What art thou to me? In thy pity, teach me to utter it. Or what am I to thee that thou demandest my love, and, if I give it not, art wroth with me, and threatenest me with grievous woes? Is it then a slight woe to love thee not? Oh! for thy mercies' sake, tell me, O Lord my God, what thou art unto me. Say unto my soul, I am thy salvation. So speak, that I may hear. Behold, Lord, my heart is before thee; open thou the ears thereof, and say unto my soul, I am thy salvation. After this voice let me haste, and take hold on thee. Hide not thy face from me. Let me die—lest I die—only let me see thy face.

Narrow is the mansion of my soul; enlarge thou it,

that thou mayest enter in. It is ruinous; repair thou it. It has that within which must offend thine eyes; I confess and know it. But who shall cleanse it? or to whom should I cry, save thee? Lord, cleanse me from my secret faults, and spare thy servant from the power of the enemy. I believe, and therefore do I speak. Lord, thou knowest. Have I not confessed against myself my transgressions unto thee, and thou, my God, hast forgiven the iniquity of my heart? I contend not in judgment with thee, who art the truth; I fear to deceive myself; lest mine iniquity lie unto itself. Therefore I contend not in judgment with thee; for if thou, Lord, shouldest mark iniquities, O Lord, who shall abide it?

Hear, Lord, my prayer; let not my soul faint under thy discipline, nor let me faint in confessing unto thee all thy mercies, whereby thou hast drawn me out of all my most evil ways, that thou mightest become a delight to me above all the allurements which I once pursued; that I may most entirely love thee, and clasp thy hand with all my affections, and thou mayest yet rescue me from every temptation, even unto the end. For lo, O Lord, my King and my God, for thy service be whatever useful thing my childhood learned; for thy service, that I speak, write, read, reckon. For thou didst grant me thy discipline, while I was learning vanities; and my sin of delighting in those vanities thou hast forgiven. In them, indeed, I learnt many a useful word, but these may as well be learned in things not vain; and that is the safe path for the steps of youth.

BOOK I

YET, Lord, to thee, the Creator and Governor of the universe, most excellent and most good, thanks were due to thee our God, even hadst thou destined for me boyhood only. For even then I was, I lived, and felt; and had an implanted providence over my well-being—a trace of that mysterious Unity whence I was derived; I guarded by the inward sense the entireness of my senses, and in these minute pursuits, and in my thoughts on things minute, I learnt to delight in truth, I hated to be deceived, had a vigorous memory, was gifted with speech, was soothed by friendship, avoided pain, baseness, ignorance. In so small a creature, what was not wonderful, not admirable? But all are gifts of my God: it was not I who gave them me; and good these are, and these together are myself. Good, then, is he that made me, and he is my good; and before him will I exult for every good which of a boy I had. For it was my sin, that not in him, but in his creatures—myself and others—I sought for pleasures, sublimities, truths, and so fell headlong into sorrows, confusions, errors. Thanks be to thee, my joy and my glory and my confidence, my God, thanks be to thee for thy gifts; but do thou preserve them to me. For so wilt thou preserve me, and those things shall be enlarged and perfected which thou hast given me, and I myself shall be with thee, since even to be thou hast given me.

BOOK I

WHAT shall I render unto the Lord, that, whilst my memory recalls these things, my soul is not affrighted at them? I will love thee, O Lord, and thank thee, and confess unto thy name; because thou hast forgiven me these so great and heinous deeds of mine. To thy grace I ascribe it, and to thy mercy, that thou hast melted away my sins as it were ice. To thy grace I ascribe also whatsoever I have not done of evil; for what might I not have done, who even loved a sin for its own sake? Yea, all I confess to have been forgiven me; both what evils I committed by my own willfulness, and what by thy guidance I committed not. What man is he, who, weighing his own infirmity, dares to ascribe his purity and innocency to his own strength; that so he should love thee the less, as if he had less needed thy mercy, whereby thou remittest sins to those that turn to thee? For whosoever, called by thee, followed thy voice, and avoided those things which he reads me recalling and confessing of myself, let him not scorn me, who being sick, was cured by that Physician, through whose aid it was that he was not, or rather was less, sick: and for this let him love thee as much, yea and more; since by whom he sees me to have been recovered from such deep consumption of sin, by him he sees himself to have been from the like consumption of sin preserved.

BOOK II

SUFFER me, I beseech thee, and give me grace to go over in my present remembrance the wanderings of my forepassed time, and to offer unto thee the sacrifice of thanksgiving. For what am I to myself without thee, but a guide to mine own downfall? Or what am I even at the best, but an infant sucking the milk thou givest, and feeding upon thee, the food that perisheth not? But what sort of man is any man, seeing he is but a man? Let now the strong and the mighty laugh at us, but let us poor and needy confess unto thee.

BOOK IV

AND now, Lord, these things are passed by, and time hath assuaged my wound. May I learn from thee, who art truth, and approach the ear of my heart unto thy mouth, that thou mayest tell me why weeping is sweet to the miserable? Hast thou, although present everywhere, cast away our misery far from thee? And thou abidest in thyself, but we are tossed about in divers trials. And yet unless we mourned in thine ears, we should have no hope left. Whence then is sweet fruit gathered from the bitterness of life, from groaning, tears, sighs, and complaints? Doth this sweeten it, that we hope thou hearest? This is true of prayer, for therein is a longing to approach unto thee. But is it also in grief for a thing lost, and the sorrow wherewith I was then overwhelmed?

BOOK IV

BEHOLD my heart, O my God, behold and see into me; for well I remember it, O my hope, who cleansest me from the impurity of such affections, directing mine eyes toward thee, and plucking my feet out of the snare. For I wondered that others, subject to death, did live, since he whom I loved, as if he should never die, was dead; and I wondered yet more that myself, who was to him a second self, could live, he being dead. Well said one of his friends, "Thou half of my soul"; for I felt that my soul and his soul were "one soul in two bodies": and therefore was my life a horror to me, because I would not live halved. And therefore perchance I feared to die, lest he whom I had much loved should die wholly.

BOOK IV

TURN us, O God of Hosts, show us thy countenance, and we shall be whole. For whithersoever the soul of man turns itself, unless toward thee, it is riveted upon sorrows, yea though it is riveted on things beautiful. And yet they, out of thee, and out of the soul, were not, unless they were from thee. They rise, and set; and by rising, they begin as it were to be; they grow, that they may be perfected; and perfected, they wax old and wither; and all grow not old, but all wither. So then when they rise and tend to be, the more quickly they grow that they may be, so much the more they haste not to be. This is the law of them. Thus much hast thou allotted them, because they are portions of things, which exist not all at once, but by passing away and succeeding, they together complete that universe, whereof they are portions. And even thus is our speech completed by signs giving forth a sound: but this again is not perfected unless one word pass away when it hath sounded its part, that another may succeed. Out of all these things let my soul praise thee, O God, Creator of all; yet let not my soul be riveted unto these things with the glue of love, through the senses of the body. For they go whither they were to go, that they might not be; and they rend her with pestilent longings, because she longs to be, yet loves to repose in what she loves. But in these things is no place of repose; they abide not, they flee; and who can follow them with the senses of the flesh? yea, who can grasp them, when they are hard by? For the sense of the flesh is slow, because it is the sense of the flesh; and thereby is it bounded. It sufficeth for that it was made for; but it sufficeth not to stay things running their course from their appointed starting place to the end appointed. For in thy word, by which they are created, they hear their decree, "hence and hitherto."

BOOK IV

FOR thou shalt light my candle, O Lord my God, thou shalt enlighten my darkness: and of thy fullness have we all received, for thou art the true light that lighteth every man that cometh into the world; for in thee there is no variableness, neither shadow of change.

BOOK IV

O Lord our God, under the shadow of thy wings let us hope; protect us, and carry us. Thou wilt carry us both when little, and even to hoar hairs wilt thou carry us; for our firmness, when it is thou, then is it firmness; but when our own, it is infirmity. Our good ever lives with thee; from which when we turn away, we are turned aside. Let us now, O Lord, return, that we may not be overturned, because with thee our good lives without any decay, which good art thou; nor need we fear, lest there be no place whither to return, because we fell from it: for through our absence, our mansion fell not—thy eternity.

BOOK IV

ACCEPT the sacrifice of my confessions from the ministry of my tongue, which thou hast formed and stirred up to confess unto thy name. Heal thou all my bones, and let them say, O Lord, who is like unto thee? For he who confesses to thee doth not teach thee what takes place within him; seeing a closed heart closes not out thy eye, nor can man's hardheartedness thrust back thy hand: for thou dissolvest it at thy will in pity or in vengeance, and nothing can hide itself from thy heat. But let my soul praise thee, that it may love thee; and let it confess thy own mercies to thee, that it may praise thee. Thy whole creation ceaseth not, nor is silent in thy praises; neither the spirit of man with voice directed unto thee, nor creation animate or inanimate, by the voice of those who meditate thereon: that so our souls may from their weariness arise toward thee, leaning on those things which thou hast created, and passing on to thyself, who madest them wonderfully; and there is refreshment and true strength.

Let the restless, the godless, depart and flee from thee; yet thou seest them, and dividest the darkness. And behold, the universe with them is fair, though they are foul. And how have they injured thee? or how have they disgraced thy government, which, from the Heaven to this lowest earth, is just and perfect? For whither fled they, when they fled from thy presence? or where dost not thou find them? But they fled, that they might not see thee seeing them, and, blinded, might stumble against thee (because thou forsakest nothing thou hast made); that the unjust, I say, might stumble upon thee, and justly be hurt; withdrawing themselves from thy gentleness, and stumbling at thy uprightness, and falling upon their own ruggedness. Ignorant, in truth, that thou art everywhere, whom no place encompasseth! and thou alone art near, even to those that remove far from thee. Let them then be turned, and seek thee; because not as they have forsaken their Creator, hast thou forsaken thy creation. Let them be turned and seek thee; and behold, thou art there in their heart, in the heart of those that confess to thee, and cast themselves upon thee, and weep in thy bosom, after all their rugged ways. Then dost thou gently wipe away their tears, and they weep the more, and joy in weeping; even for that thou, Lord,—not man of flesh and blood, but—thou, Lord, who madest them, re-makest and comfortest them. But where was I, when I was seeking thee? And thou wert before me, but I had gone away from thee; nor did I find myself, how much less thee!

BOOK V

O thou, my hope from my youth, where wert thou to me, and whither wert thou gone? Hadst not thou created me, and separated me from the beasts of the field, and fowls of the air? Thou hadst made me wiser, yet did I walk in darkness, and in slippery places, and sought thee abroad out of myself, and found not the God of my heart; and had come into the depths of the sea, and distrusted and despaired of ever finding truth.

BOOK VI

THOU wert with me; I sighed, and thou heardest me; I wavered, and thou didst guide me; I wandered through the broad way of the world, and thou didst not forsake me.

I panted after honors, gains, marriage; and thou deridedst me. In these desires I underwent most bitter crosses, thou being the more gracious, the less thou sufferedst aught to grow sweet to me, which was not thou. Behold my heart, O Lord, who wouldest I should remember all this, and confess to thee. Let my soul cleave unto thee, now that thou hast freed it from that fast-holding bird-lime of death. How wretched was it! and thou didst irritate the feeling of its wound, that forsaking all else, it might be converted unto thee, who art above all, and without whom all things would be nothing; be converted, and be healed.

BOOK VI

BUT thou, Lord, abidest forever, yet not forever art thou angry with us; because thou pitiest our dust and ashes, and it was pleasing in thy sight to reform my deformities; and by inward goads didst thou rouse me, that I should be ill at ease, until thou wert manifested to my inward sight. Thus, by the secret hand of thy medicining was my swelling abated, and the troubled and bedimmed eyesight of my mind, by the smarting anointings of healthful sorrows, was from day to day healed.

And thou, willing first to show me how thou resistest the proud, but givest grace unto the humble, and by how great an act of thy mercy thou hadst traced out to men the way of humility, in that thy Word was made flesh, and dwelt among men.

BOOK VII

FOR, thou art righteous, O Lord, but we have sinned and committed iniquity, and have done wickedly, and thy hand is grown heavy upon us, and we are justly delivered over unto that ancient sinner, the king of death; because he persuaded our will to be like his will, whereby he abode not in thy truth. What shall wretched man do? who shall deliver him from the body of this death, but only thy grace, through Jesus Christ our Lord, whom thou hast begotten co-eternal, and formedst in the beginning of thy ways, in whom the prince of this world found nothing worthy of death, yet killed he him.

BOOK VII

UP, Lord, and do; stir us up, and recall us; kindle and draw us; inflame, grow sweet unto us; let us now love, let us run.

BOOK VIII

O my God, let me, with thanksgiving, remember, and confess unto thee thy mercies on me. Let my bones be bedewed with thy love, and let them say unto thee, who is like unto thee, O Lord? Thou hast broken my bonds in sunder. I will offer unto thee the sacrifice of thanksgiving. And how thou hast broken them, I will declare; and all who worship thee, when they hear this, shall say, "Blessed be the Lord, in Heaven and in earth, great and wonderful is his name." Thy words had stuck fast in my heart, and I was hedged round about on all sides by thee.

BOOK VIII

O Lord, I am thy servant; I am thy servant, and the son of thy handmaid: thou hast broken my bonds in sunder. I will offer to thee the sacrifice of praise. Let my heart and my tongue praise thee; yea, let all my bones say, O Lord, who is like unto thee? Let them say, and answer thou me, and say unto my soul, I am thy salvation. Who am I, and what am I? What evil have not been either my deeds, or if not my deeds, my words, or if not my words, my will? But thou, O Lord, art good and merciful, and thy right hand had respect unto the depth of my death, and from the bottom of my heart emptied that abyss of corruption. And this thy whole gift was, to will what I willed, and to will what thou willedst. But where through all those years, and out of what low and deep recess was my free will called forth in a moment, whereby to submit my neck to thy easy yoke, and my shoulders unto thy light burden, O Christ Jesus, my Helper and my Redeemer? How sweet did it at once become to me, to want the sweetnesses of those toys! and what I feared to be parted from was now a joy to part with. For thou didst cast them forth from me, thou true and highest sweetness. Thou castest them forth, and for them enteredst in thyself, sweeter than all pleasure, though not to flesh and blood; brighter than all light, but more hidden than all depths, higher than all honor, but not to the high in their own conceits. Now was my soul free from the biting cares of canvassing and getting, and weltering in filth, and scratching off the itch of lust. And my infant tongue spake freely to thee, my brightness, and my riches, and my health, the Lord my God.

BOOK IX

LET me know thee, O Lord, who knowest me: let me know thee, as I am known. Power of my soul, enter into it, and fit it for thee, that thou mayest have and hold it without spot or wrinkle. This is my hope, therefore do I speak; and in this hope do I rejoice, when I rejoice healthfully. Other things of this life are the less to be sorrowed for, the more they are sorrowed for; and the more to be sorrowed for, the less men sorrow for them. For behold, thou lovest the truth, and he that doth it, cometh to the light. This would I do in my heart before thee in confession: and in my writing, before many witnesses.

And from thee, O Lord, unto whose eyes the abyss of man's conscience is naked, what could be hidden in me though I would not confess it? For I should hide thou from me, not me from thee. But now, for that my groaning is witness, that I am displeased with myself, thou shinest out, and art pleasing, and beloved, and longed for; that I may be ashamed of myself, and renounce myself, and choose thee, and neither please thee nor myself, but in thee. To thee therefore, O Lord, am I open, whatever I am; and with what fruit I confess unto thee, I have said. Nor do I it with words and sounds of the flesh, but with the words of my soul, and the cry of the thought which thy ear knoweth. For when I am evil, then to confess to thee is nothing else than to be displeased with myself; but when holy, nothing else than not to ascribe it to myself: because thou, O Lord, blessest the godly, but first thou justifieth him when ungodly. My confession then, O my God, in thy sight, is made silently, and not silently. For in sound, it is silent; in affection, it cries aloud. For neither do I utter anything right unto men, which thou hast not before heard from me; nor dost thou hear any such thing from me, which thou hast not first said unto me.

BOOK X

FOR it is no mean fruit, O Lord my God, that by many thanks should be given to thee on our behalf, and thou be by many entreated for us. Let the brotherly mind love in me what thou teachest is to be loved, and lament in me what thou teachest is to be lamented. Let a brotherly, not a stranger, mind, not that of the strange children, whose mouth talketh of vanity, and their right hand is a right hand of iniquity, but that brotherly mind which when it approveth, rejoiceth for me, and when it disapproveth me, is sorry for me; because whether it approveth or disapproveth, it loveth me. To such will I discover myself: they will breathe freely at my good deeds, sigh for my ill. My good deeds are thine appointments, and thy gifts; my evil ones are my offenses, and thy judgments. Let them breathe freely at the one, sigh at the other; and let hymns and weeping go up into thy sight, out of the hearts of my brethren, thy censers. And do thou, O Lord, be pleased with the incense of thy holy temple, have mercy upon me according to thy great mercy for thine own name's sake; and no ways forsaking what thou hast begun, perfect my imperfections.

BOOK X

FOR thou, Lord, dost judge me: because, although no man knoweth the things of a man, but the spirit of a man which is in him, yet is there something of man, which neither the spirit of man that is in him, itself knoweth. But thou, Lord, knowest all of him, who hast made him. Yet I, though in thy sight I despise myself, and account myself dust and ashes; yet know I something of thee, which I know not of myself. And truly, now we see through a glass darkly, not face to face as yet. So long therefore as I be absent from thee, I am more present with myself than with thee; and yet know I thee that thou art in no ways passible; but I, what temptations I can resist, what I cannot, I know not.

And there is hope, because thou art faithful, who wilt not suffer us to be tempted above that we are able; but wilt with the temptation also make a way to escape, that we may be able to bear it. I will confess then what I know of myself, I will confess also what I know not of myself. And that because what I do know of myself, I know by thy shining upon me; and what I know not of myself, so long know I not it, until my darkness be made as the noon-day in thy countenance.

Not with doubting, but with assured consciousness, do I love thee, Lord. Thou hast stricken my heart with thy word, and I loved thee. Yea also Heaven, and earth, and all that therein is, behold, on every side they bid me love thee; nor cease to say so unto all, that they may be without excuse. But more deeply wilt thou have mercy on whom thou wilt have mercy, and wilt have compassion on whom thou hast had compassion; else in deaf ears do the Heaven and the earth speak thy praises. But what do I love, when I love thee? not beauty of bodies, nor the fair harmony of time, nor the brightness of the light, so gladsome to our eyes, nor sweet melodies of varied songs, nor the fragrant smell of flowers, and ointments, and spices, not manna and honey, not limbs acceptable to embracements of flesh. None of these I love, when I love my God; and yet I love a kind of light, and melody, and fragrance, and meat, and embracement when I love my God, the light, melody, fragrance, meat, embracement of my inner man: where there shineth unto my soul what space cannot contain, and there soundeth what time beareth not away, and there smelleth what breathing disperseth not, and there tasteth what eating diminisheth not, and there clingeth what satiety divorceth not. This is it which I love when I love my God.

BOOK X

GREAT is the power of memory, a fearful thing, O my God, a deep and boundless manifoldness; and this thing is the mind, and this am I myself. What am I then, O my God? What nature am I? A life various and manifold, and exceeding immense. Behold in the plains and caves and caverns of my memory, innumerable and innumerably full of innumerable kinds of things, either through images, as all bodies; or by actual presence, as the arts; or by certain notions or impressions, as the affections of the mind, which, even when the mind doth not feel, the memory retaineth, while yet whatsoever is in the memory is also in the mind—over all these do I run, I fly; I dive on this side and on that, as far as I can, and there is no end. So great is the force of memory, so great the force of life, even in the mortal life of man. What shall I do then, O thou my true life, my God? I will pass even beyond this power of mine which is called memory: yea, I will pass beyond it, that I may approach unto thee, O sweet Light. What sayest thou to me? See, I am mounting up through my mind toward thee who abidest above me. Yea, I now will pass beyond this power of mine which is called memory, desirous to arrive at thee, whence thou mayest be arrived at; and to cleave unto thee, whence one may cleave unto thee. For even beasts and birds have memory; else could they not return to their dens and nests, nor many other things they are used unto: nor indeed could they be used to anything, but by memory. I will pass then beyond memory also, that I may arrive at him who hath separated me from the four-footed beasts and made me wiser than the fowls of the air, I will pass beyond memory also, and where shall I find thee, thou truly good and certain sweetness? And where shall I find thee? If I find thee without my memory, then do I not retain thee in my memory. And how shall I find thee, if I remember thee not?

BOOK X

TOO late loved I thee, O thou Beauty of ancient days, yet ever new! too late I loved thee! And behold, thou wert within, and I abroad, and there I searched for thee; deformed I, plunging amid those fair forms which thou hadst made. Thou wert with me, but I was not with thee. Things held me far from thee, which, unless they were in thee, were not at all. Thou calledst and shoutedst and burstest my deafness. Thou flashedst, shonest, and scatteredst my blindness. Thou breathedst odors, and I drew in breath and pant for thee. I tasted and hunger and thirst. Thou touchedst me, and I burned for thy peace.

When I shall with my whole self cleave to thee, I shall nowhere have sorrow or labor; and my life shall wholly live, as wholly full of thee. But now since whom thou fillest, thou liftest up, because I am not full of thee I am a burden to myself. Lamentable joys strive with joyous sorrows: and on which side is the victory, I know not. Woe is me! Lord, have pity on me. My evil sorrows strive with my good joys; and on which side is the victory, I know not. Woe is me! Lord, have pity on me. Woe is me! lo! I hide not my wounds; thou art the Physician, I the sick; thou merciful, I miserable. Is not the life of man upon earth all trial? Who wishes for troubles and difficulties? Thou commandest them to be endured, not to be loved. No man loves what he endures, though he love to endure. For though he rejoices that he endures, he had rather there were nothing for him to endure. In adversity I long for prosperity, in prosperity I fear adversity. What middle place is there betwixt these two, where the life of man is not all trial? Woe to the prosperities of the world, once and again, through fear of adversity, and corruption of joy! Woe to the adversities of the world, once and again, and the third time, from the longing for prosperity, and because adversity itself is a hard thing, and lest it shatter endurance. Is not the life of man upon earth all trial: without any interval?

And all my hope is nowhere but in thy exceeding great mercy. Give what thou enjoinest, and enjoin what thou wilt.

BOOK X

AND thou knowest how far thou hast already changed me, who first healedst me of the lust of vindicating myself, that so thou mightest forgive all the rest of my iniquities, and heal all my infirmities, and redeem my life from corruption, and crown me with mercy and pity, and satisfy my desire with good things: who didst curb my pride with thy fear, and tame my neck to thy yoke. And now I bear it and it is light unto me, because so hast thou promised, and hast made it; and verily so it was, and I knew it not, when I feared to take it.

BOOK X

HOW then do I seek thee, O Lord? For when I seek thee, my God, I seek a happy life. I will seek thee, that my soul may live. For my body liveth by my soul; and my soul by thee. How then do I seek a happy life, seeing I have it not, until I can say, where I ought to say it, "It is enough"?

BOOK X

O Lord my God, give ear unto my prayer, and let thy mercy hearken unto my desire: because it is anxious not for myself alone, but would serve brotherly charity; and thou seest my heart, that so it is. I would sacrifice to thee the service of my thought and tongue; do thou give me, what I may offer thee. For I am poor and needy, thou rich to all that call upon thee; who, inaccessible to care, carest for us. Circumcise from all rashness and all lying both my inward and outward lips: let thy Scriptures be my pure delights: let me not be deceived in them, nor deceive out of them. Lord, hearken and pity, O Lord my God, Light of the blind, and Strength of the weak; yea also Light of those that see, and Strength of the strong; hearken unto my soul, and hear it crying out of the depths. For if thine ears be not with us in the depths also, whither shall we go? whither cry? The day is thine, and the night is thine; at thy beck the moments flee by. Grant thereof a space for our meditations in the hidden things of thy law, and close it not against us who knock. For not in vain wouldest thou have the darksome secrets of so many pages written; nor are those forests without their harts which retire therein and range and walk; feed, lie down, and ruminate. Perfect me, O Lord, and reveal them unto me. Behold, thy voice is my joy; thy voice exceedeth the abundance of pleasures. Give what I love: for I do love; and this hast thou given: forsake not thy own gifts, nor despise thy green herb that thirsteth. Let me confess unto thee whatsoever I shall find in thy books, and hear the voice of praise, and drink in thee, and meditate on the wonderful things out of thy law; even from the beginning, wherein thou madest the Heaven and the earth, unto the everlasting reigning of thy holy city with thee.

Lord, have mercy on me, and hear my desire. For it is not, I deem, of the earth, not of gold and silver, and precious stones, or gorgeous apparel, or honors and offices, or the pleasures of the flesh, or necessaries for the body and for this life of our pilgrimage: all which shall be added unto those that seek thy kingdom and thy righteousness. Behold, O Lord my God, wherein is my desire. The wicked have told me of delights, but not such as thy law, O Lord. Behold, wherein is my desire. Behold, Father, behold, and see and approve; and be it pleasing in the sight of thy mercy, that I may find grace before thee, that the inward parts of thy words be opened to me knocking.

BOOK XI

O Lord my God, what a depth is that recess of thy mysteries, and how far from it have the consequences of my transgressions cast me! Heal mine eyes, that I may share the joy of thy light.

BOOK XI

MY heart, O Lord, touched with the words of thy holy Scripture, is much busied, amid this poverty of my life. And therefore most times is the poverty of human understanding copious in words, because inquiring hath more to say than discovering, and demanding is longer than obtaining, and our hand that knocks hath more work to do than our hand that receives. We hold the promise, who shall make it null? If God be for us, who can be against us? Ask, and ye shall have; seek, and ye shall find; knock, and it shall be opened unto you. For everyone that asketh, receiveth; and he that seeketh, findeth; and to him that knocketh, shall it be opened. These be thine own promises: and who need fear to be deceived, when the truth promiseth?

BOOK XII

I call upon thee, O my God, my mercy, who createdst me, and forgettest not me, forgetting thee. I call thee into my soul, which, by the longing thyself inspirest into her, thou preparest for thee. Forsake me not now calling upon thee, whom thou preventedst before I called, and urgedst me with much variety of repeated calls, that I would hear thee from afar, and be converted, and call upon thee, that calledst after me; for thou, Lord, blottedst out all my evil deservings, so as not to repay into my hands, wherewith I fell from thee; and thou hast prevented all my well deservings, so as to repay the work of thy hands wherewith thou madest me; because before I was, thou wert; nor was I any thing, to which thou mightest grant to be; and yet behold, I am, out of thy goodness, preventing all this which thou hast made me, and whereof thou hast made me. For neither hadst thou need of me, nor am I any such good, as to be helpful unto thee, my Lord and God; not in serving thee, as though thou wouldest tire in working; or lest thy power might be less, if lacking my service: nor cultivating thy service, as a land, that must remain uncultivated, unless I cultivated thee: but serving and worshiping thee, that I might receive a well-being from thee, from whom it comes, that I have a being capable of well-being.

BOOK XIII

WE are inflamed, by thy gift we are kindled; and are carried upwards; we glow inwardly, and go forwards. We ascend thy ways that be in our heart, and sing a song of degrees; we glow inwardly with thy fire, with thy good fire, and we go; because we go upwards to the peace of Jerusalem: for gladdened was I in those who said unto me, We will go up to the house of the Lord. There hath thy good pleasure placed us, that we may desire nothing else, but to abide there forever.

BOOK XIII

BUT the souls that thirst after thee, and that appear before thee (being by other bounds divided from the society of the sea), thou waterest by a sweet spring, that the earth may bring forth her fruit, and thou, Lord God, so commanding, our soul may bud forth works of mercy according to their kind, loving our neighbor in the relief of his bodily necessities, having seed in itself according to its likeness, when from feeling of our infirmity, we compassionate so as to relieve the needy; helping them, as we would be helped, if we were in like need; not only in things easy, as in herb yielding seed, but also in the protection of our assistance, with our best strength, like the tree yielding fruit: that is, well-doing in rescuing him that suffers wrong, from the hand of the powerful, and giving him the shelter of protection, by the mighty strength of just judgment.

So, Lord, so, I beseech thee, let there spring up, as thou doest, as thou givest cheerfulness and ability, let truth spring out of the earth, and righteousness look down from Heaven, and let there be lights in the firmament. Let us break our bread to the hungry, and bring the houseless poor to our house. Let us clothe the naked, and despise not those of our own flesh. Which fruits having sprung out of the earth, see it is good: and let our temporary light break forth; and ourselves, from this lower fruitfulness of action, arriving at the delightfulness of contemplation, obtaining the word of life above, appear like lights in the world, cleaving to the firmament of thy Scripture.

BOOK XIII

THANKS to thee, O Lord. We behold the Heaven and earth, whether the corporeal part, superior and inferior, or the spiritual and corporeal creature; and in the adorning of these parts, whereof the universal pile of the world, or rather the universal creation, doth consist, we see light made, and divided from the darkness. We see the firmament of Heaven, whether that primary body of the world, between the spiritual upper waters and the inferior corporeal waters, or (since this also is called Heaven) this space of air through which wander the fowls of Heaven, betwixt those waters which are in vapors borne above them, and in clear nights distill down in dew; and those heavier waters which flow along the earth. We behold a face of waters gathered together in the fields of the sea; and the dry land both void, and formed so as to be visible and harmonized, yea and the matter of herbs and trees. We behold the lights shining from above, the sun to suffice for the day, the moon and the stars to cheer the night; and that by all these, times should be marked and signified. We behold on all sides a moist element, replenished with fishes, beasts, and birds; because the grossness of the air, which bears up the flights of birds, thickeneth itself by the exhalation of the waters. We behold the face of the earth decked out with earthly creatures, and man, created after thy image and likeness, even through that thy very image and likeness (that is the power of reason and understanding), set over all irrational creatures. And as in his soul there is one power which has dominion by directing, another made subject, that it might obey; so was there for the man, corporeally also, made a woman, who in the mind of her reasonable understanding should have a parity of nature. . . . These things we behold, and they are severally good, and altogether very good.

Let thy works praise thee, that we may love thee; and let us love thee, that thy works may praise thee, which from time have beginning and ending, rising and setting, growth and decay, form and privation. They have then their succession of morning and evening, part secretly, part apparently; for they were made of nothing, by thee, not of thee; not of any matter not thine, or that was before, but of matter concreated (that is, at the same time created by thee), because to its state without form, thou without any interval of time didst give form. For seeing the matter of Heaven and earth is one thing, and the form another, thou madest the matter of merely nothing, but the form of the world out of the matter without form: yet both together, so that the form should follow the matter, without any interval of delay.

BOOK XIII

O Lord God, give peace unto us: (for thou hast given us all things) the peace of rest, the peace of the sabbath, which hath no evening. For all this most goodly array of things very good, having finished their courses, is to pass away, for in them there was morning and evening.

BOOK XIII

F O U R T E E N

Prayers from Sermons, Commentaries, and Tractates

DIRECTING my purpose by this rule of faith, so far as I have been able, by all that you have created in me, I have sought you, and have desired to see with my understanding what I believed; and I have argued and labored much. O my Lord, my God, my hope, hear me, so that weariness may not diminish my will to seek you, but that I may always ardently seek your face. Give me the strength to seek you as you have made me find you, and have given me hope of finding you more and more. My strength and my weakness are in your hands; preserve the one and heal the other. My knowledge and my ignorance are in your hands; where you have opened yourself to me, receive my entering in; where you have been closed to me, open to my knocking. Let me remember you, understand you, love you. Increase these things in me, until you restore me wholly.

ON THE TRINITY

"YEA, though I walk in the midst of the shadow of death." Yea, though I walk in the midst of this life, which is the shadow of death. "I will fear no evil, for thou art with me." I will fear no evil, for thou dwellest in my heart by faith: and thou art now with me, that after the shadow of death I too may be with thee. "Thy rod and thy staff, they have comforted me." Thy discipline, like a rod for a flock of sheep, and like a staff for children of some size, and growing out of the natural into spiritual life, they have not been grievous to me; rather have they comforted me: because thou art mindful of me.

"Thou hast prepared a table in my sight, against them that trouble me." Now after the rod, whereby, whilst a little one, and living the natural life, I was brought up among the flock in the pastures; after that rod, I say, when I began to be under the staff, thou hast prepared a table in my sight, that I should no more be fed as a babe with milk, but being older should take meat, strengthened against them that trouble me. "Thou hast fattened my head with oil." Thou hast gladdened my mind with spiritual joy. "And thy inebriating cup, how excellent is it!" And thy cup yielding forgetfulness of former vain delights, how excellent is it!

ON PSALM 23

"THAT thy beloved may be delivered: save me with thy right hand, and hearken unto me." With thy right hand save me, Lord: so save me as that at the right hand I may stand. Not any safety temporal I require, in this matter thy will be done. For a time what is good for us we are utterly ignorant: for "what we should pray for as we ought we know not": but "save me with thy right hand," so that even if in this time I suffer sundry tribulations, when the night of all tribulations hath been spent, on the right hand I may be found among the sheep, not on the left hand among the goats. "And hearken unto me." Because now I am deserving that which thou art willing to give; not "with the words of my transgressions" I am crying through the day, so that thou hearken not, and "in the night so that thou hearken not," and that not for folly to me, but truly for my warning, by adding savor from the valley of salt pits, so that in tribulation I may know what to ask: but I ask life everlasting; therefore hearken unto me, because thy right hand I ask.

ON PSALM 60

"WILT not thou, O God, that hast driven us back? And wilt not thou, O God, march forth in our powers?" Wilt not thou lead us down, that hast driven us back? But wherefore "hast driven us back"? Because thou hast destroyed us. Wherefore hast destroyed us? Because angry thou hast been, and hast had pity on us. Thou therefore wilt lead down, that hast driven back; thou, O God, that wilt not march forth in our powers, wilt lead down. What is, "wilt not march forth in our powers"? The world is to rage, the world is to tread us down, there is to be a heap of witnesses, builded of the spilled blood of martyrs, and the raging heathen are to say, "Where is the God of them?" Then "Thou wilt not march forth in our powers": against them thou wilt not show thyself, thou wilt not show thy power, such as thou hast shown in David, in Moses, in Joshua the son of Nun, when to their might the Gentiles yielded, and when the slaughter had been ended, and the great laying waste repaired, into the land which thou promisedst thou leddest in thy people. This thing then thou wilt not do, "Thou wilt not march forth in our powers," but within thou wilt work. . . .

Thou therefore, O God, that wilt not march forth in our powers. "Give to us aid from tribulation, and vain is the safety of man."

ON PSALM 60

"BLESS our God, ye nations." Behold, there have been driven back they that are bitter, reckoning hath been made with them: some have been converted, some have continued proud. Let not them terrify you that grudge the Gentiles Gospel grace: now hath come the seed of Abraham, in whom are blessed all nations. Bless ye him in whom ye are blessed, "Bless our God, ye nations: and hear ye the voice of his praise." Praise not yourselves, but praise him. What is the voice of his praise? That by his grace we are whatever of good we are. . . .

He hath set my soul unto life, he guideth the feet that they stumble not, be not moved and given unto motion; he maketh us to live, he maketh us to persevere even unto the end, in order that for everlasting we may live. . . .

"For thou hast proved us, O God; thou hast fired us as silver is fired." Hast not fired us like hay, but like silver: by applying to us fire, thou hast not turned us into ashes, but thou hast washed off uncleanness, "thou hast fired us, as silver is fired." And see in what manner God is wroth against them, whose soul he hath set unto life.

ON PSALM 66

WITHIN may I keep thy love, it shall not be on the surface, in my marrow it shall be that I love thee. For there is nothing more inward than our marrow: the bones are more inward than the flesh, the marrow is more inward than those same bones.

ON PSALM 66

WHEN then he proposed, "Praise God in his saints," to whom said he this, save to themselves? And in whom are they to praise God, save in themselves? For ye, saith he, are "his saints"; ye are "his strength," but that which he wrought in you; ye are "his mighty works, and the multitude of his greatness," which he hath wrought and set forth in you. Ye are "trumpet, psaltery, harp, timbrel, choir, strings, and organ, cymbals of jubilation sounding well," because sounding in harmony. All these are ye: let naught that is vile, naught that is transitory, naught that is ludicrous, be here thought of. And since to savor of the flesh is death, "let every spirit praise the Lord."

ON PSALM 150

O that I might speak only in preaching thy word and in praising thee! Not only should I so flee from sin, but I should earn good desert, however much I so spake. For a man blessed of thee would not enjoin a sin upon his own true son in the faith, to whom he wrote, "Preach the word: be instant in season, out of season." Are we to say that he has not spoken much, who was not silent about thy word,

O Lord, not only in season but out of season? But, therefore, it was not much because it was only what was necessary. Set me free, O God, from that multitude of speech which I suffer inwardly in my soul, wretched as it is in thy sight and flying for refuge to thy mercy; for I am not silent in thoughts even when silent in words. And if indeed I thought of nothing save what pleased thee, certainly I would not ask thee to set me free from such multitude of speech. But many are my thoughts, such as thou knowest "thoughts of man, since they are vain." Grant to me not to consent to them; and if ever they delight me, nevertheless to condemn them and not to dwell in them, as though I slumbered. Nor let them so prevail in me, as that anything in my acts should proceed from them; but at least let my opinions, let my conscience, be safe from them under thy protection. When the wise man spake of thee in his book, which is now called by the special name of Ecclesiasticus, "We speak," he said, "much, and yet come short; and in sum of words, he is all." When, therefore, we shall have come to thee, these very many things that we speak, and yet come short, will cease; and thou, as one, wilt remain "all in all." And we shall say one thing without end, in praising thee in one, ourselves also made one in thee.

ON THE TRINITY

O great is your patience, Lord, full of compassion and gracious, slow to anger, plenteous in mercy, and true; you who make your sun rise upon the good and the evil alike and who send rain upon both just and unjust; you who do not will the death of the sinner, but rather that he return and truly live; you, who reproving us in parts, give its proper place to repentance, so that having abandoned wickedness, they may believe in you, O Lord; who by your patience lead us to repentance, although many because of the hardness of their hearts and their impenitence store up wrath in themselves against the day of wrath and of the revelation of your righteous judgment; you, who will judge every man according to his works; you, who in the day when a man has returned from his iniquity to your mercy and truth, will forget all his iniquities: do stand before us, grant to us that through our ministry, by which you have been pleased to refute execrable and all too horrible errors, as many have already been liberated, may many also still be liberated, and whether through the sacrament of your holy baptism, or through the sacrifice of a broken spirit and a contrite and humbled heart, or in the sorrow of repentance, may they deserve to receive the remission of their sins and blasphemies, by which through ignorance they have offended you. For nothing is of any help except your incomparable mercy and strength, the truth of your baptism, and the keys of the kingdom of Heaven in your holy Church. We must not despair of men as long as by your patience they live on this earth, even those who know how great an evil it is to think or to say such things about you, and continue to do so because it is expedient to do so in order to attain or to hold onto temporal, worldly success, when we see that, rebuked by your reproaches, they flee to your ineffable goodness and prefer to all the enticements of the life of this world the heavenly and eternal life to come.

CONCERNING THE NATURE OF GOD

WE cry, therefore, with the spirit of charity. Until we come to the inheritance in which we are to stay forever, let us abide here in the love which becomes the free-born, not with the fear which identifies slaves, and let us be patient as we must be in our suffering. We cry so long as we are poor, until we are rewarded with that inheritance which makes us rich. See what great pledges of that reward we have received, in the person of Jesus Christ, who to make us rich made himself poor, who himself was exalted in the riches which are above, and in the person of that one who could breathe into our hearts holy longings, the Holy Spirit. Let us be among those poor, still believing, though not yet beholding; still hoping, though not yet enjoying; still sighing in desire, though not yet reigning in joy; still hungering and thirsting, not yet satisfied. Of these poor, "the patience shall never perish": not that there will be patience there also, where there should not be, but it will not in one sense ever perish, meaning it will not be unfruitful. Rather, its fruit it will have forever, therefore it shall not ever perish. For he who labors in vain, when the hope fails for which he has labored, says with good reason, "I have labored in vain." But he who receives the promise of his labor says, congratulating himself, "I have not labored in vain." Labor, then, is said not to perish or be lost, not because it lasts perpetually, but because it is not spent in vain. So also the patience of the poor of Christ, who still are to be made rich as heirs of Christ, shall never perish, not because there also we shall be commanded to bear everything with patience, but because in return for bearing so much with patience, we shall enjoy eternal bliss. He will put no end to our everlasting joy, he who gives our will its temporal patience, because both the one and the other, the patience and its reward, are bestowed by him as gifts in return for our charity, from him whose gift that charity is also.

ON PATIENCE

MY mouth will speak the praise of the Lord, of the Lord through whom all things have been made and who has been made in the midst of all things; who is the Revealer of his Father, the Creator of his Mother; who is the Son of God through his Father without a mother, the Son of man through his Mother without a father. He is great as the day of the angels is great, and small as the day of men, the Word of God before all time, the Word made flesh at a suitable time. Maker of the sun, he is made under the sun. Disposer of all ages in the bosom of the Father, he consecrates this day in the womb of his Mother. In him he remains, from her he goes forth. Creator of Heaven and earth, he was born on earth under Heaven. Unspeakably wise, he is wise speechless. Filling the world, he lies in a manger. Ruler of the stars, he nurses at his Mother's bosom. He is both great in the nature of God and small in the form of a servant, but in such a way that his greatness is not diminished by his smallness, nor his smallness overwhelmed by his greatness. For he did not desert his divine works when he took to himself human parts. Nor did he cease to reach from end to end mightily, and to order all things sweetly, when, having put on the infirmity of the flesh, he was received into the Virgin's womb, not confined therein. Thus the food of wisdom was not taken away from the angels, and we were to taste how sweet is the Lord.

A CHRISTMAS SERMON

O food and bread of angels, the angels are filled by you, are satisfied by you, but not to the point of satiety. They live by you; they have wisdom by you. By you they are blessed. Where are you for my sake? In a mean lodging, in a manger. For whom? He who rules the stars sucks at the breast. He who speaks in the bosom of the Father is silent in the Mother's lap. But he will speak when he reaches a suitable age, and will fulfill for us the Gospel. For our sakes he will suffer, for us he will die. As an example of our reward, he will rise again. He will ascend into Heaven before the eyes of his disciples, and he will come from Heaven to judge the world. Behold him lying in the manger; he is reduced to tininess, yet he has not lost anything of himself. He has accepted what was not his, but he remains what he was. Look, we have the infant Christ; let us grow with him.

A CHRISTMAS SERMON

TO you do we betake ourselves, and with your help all will be well with us. For things go badly for us when left to ourselves. Because we have left you, you have left us to ourselves. Let us, then, be found in you, for in ourselves we are lost. Lord, you are our refuge. Why, then, brethren, should we doubt that the Lord will make us gentle, if we give ourselves up to be tamed by him? You have tamed the lion which you did not make; shall he not tame you, he who made you? For from where did you get the power to tame such savage beasts? Are you their equal in bodily strength? By what power, then, have you been able to tame great beasts? Even the beasts of burden, as they are called, are by nature wild. In their untamed state they are no use to us, but because we have never known them except in the hands and under the bridle and power of men, do we imagine that they must have been born in this tame state? Now let us think of beasts of unquestionably savage kind. "The lion roareth, who does not fear?" Where, then, and in what do you find yourself stronger than the lion? Not in strength of body, but in the interior reason of the mind. You are stronger than the lion, in that in which you were made after the image of God. Well, then, shall the image of God tame a wild beast and shall God himself not tame his own image?

SERMONS ON THE NEW TESTAMENT

LORD, you have become our refuge from generation to generation. In the first and second generations, you were our refuge. You were our refuge so that we might be born who before were not. You were our refuge so that we might be born anew who were evil. You were a refuge to feed those that did forsake you. You are a refuge to raise up and direct your children. You are our refuge. We will not turn back from you for you have delivered us from all our evils and filled us with your own good things. You give good things now; you deal softly with us so that we will not be wearied in the way. You correct and chastise and strike and direct us so that we may not wander from the way. Therefore, whether you deal softly with us so that we will not be wearied in the way, or chastise us so that we do not wander from the way, you are our refuge, O Lord.

SERMONS ON THE NEW TESTAMENT

O Lord my God, O Lord our God, make us happy in you so that we may come to you. We do not want our happiness to come from gold or silver or land, from these earthly and most vain and transitory goods of this perishable life.

Do not let our mouths speak vanity. Make us happy in you, seeing and knowing that we shall never lose you. When we shall once have hold of you, we shall neither lose you nor be lost ourselves. Make us happy in you, because happy are the people whose Lord is their God. Nor will God be angry if we say of him, he is our estate. For we read that "the Lord is the portion of my inheritance." A grand thing, brethren, that we are his inheritance and that he is ours, seeing that we cultivate his service and he cultivates us. It is no derogation of his honor to say that he cultivates us. Because if we cultivate him as our God, he cultivates us as his field. And, so that you may know that he cultivates us, hear him whom he has sent to us: "I am the vine, you are the branches, my father is the husbandman."

SERMONS ON THE NEW TESTAMENT

O that there were a heart panting in any measure for that ineffable glory! O that we felt with groans our state as pilgrims and foreigners, and did not so love the world, but rather, at the door of him who called us, did with pious mind keep up a perpetual knocking! Desire is the heart's bosom and lap; we shall receive, if we stretch out our desire as widely as we can.

ON THE GOSPEL OF JOHN

TELL me, my Lord, what to tell your servants and my fellow servants. The apostle Thomas had you before his eyes to question you, yet for all that he would not have understood you if he had not had you in his heart. I question you because I know you are high above me. I question you insofar as I am able to pour out my soul on high where, though I may not hear you speak, I do hear you teach. Tell me, I beseech you, how do you go to yourself? It cannot be that you left yourself to come to us, for in truth you did not come from yourself, but the Father sent you. I know that you did empty yourself, but it was by taking the form of a servant, not by giving up the form of God to return to it again, nor by losing it to receive it back again. And yet you did come, not only within the range of the eyes of our flesh, but even within the touch of our human hands. How, but in the flesh? By means of flesh you came, yet remained where you were. By the same means you returned, still remaining where you came from. If, then, by this means you did come and go, by the same means surely not only are you the way and means for us to come to you, but were also the way for you yourself to come and to return. And when you did go to life, which is to say yourself, you raised that same flesh of yours from death to life.

ON THE GOSPEL OF JOHN

LET them hear you, and let them come to you. Let them learn from you to be meek and lowly, those who seek your mercy and truth, by living in and for you, not in and for themselves. Let him hear this, him laboring and laden, weighed down by his burden, not so much as to dare to lift up his eyes to Heaven, that sinner who beats his breast, and must come from so far off. Let him hear, the centurion who is not worthy that you should enter under his roof. Let him hear, Zaccheus, chief of the publicans, always restoring and magnifying the gains of damnable sins. Let her hear, the woman in the city, a sinner, so much the more full of tears at your feet, the more distant she had been from your steps. Let them hear, the harlots and publicans who enter into the kingdom of Heaven ahead of the scribes and Pharisees. Let them hear, every such person with whom your meeting and feasting was cast in your teeth as a charge against you—as though these were healthy persons who did not need a physician, whereas in fact you came not to summon the righteous, but to call sinners to repent. All of these people, when they are converted to you, easily grow meek and are humbled before you. They are aware of their most unrighteous life, and of your great mercy, knowing that where sin has once abounded, grace has then been all the more abundant.

ON HOLY VIRGINITY

O saving teaching! Teacher and Lord of mortals, who was our pledge unto death and the answer to pride, he would not teach what he himself was not, he would not bid others do what he himself would not do. I see you, O good Jesus, with the eyes of faith, which you have opened for me, as if you were standing in an assembly of all of the human race, crying out and saying, Come to me and learn from me. Why, I beseech you, through whom all things were made, O Son of God, who nonetheless was made as one of us, O Son of man, why do we come to you? To learn what do we come to you? Because I am meek, he says, and lowly of heart. Is it to this that all the treasures of wisdom and knowledge hidden in you are brought, so that we can learn this from you, a great thing made small enough for us to understand: that nothing could be learned at all unless it were brought to pass by you, who are so great? So indeed it is. For in no other way can rest be found that is true rest for the soul . . . except when the unquiet swelling has been brought down, that swelling which made the soul great to. itself when it was not sound in and by you.

ON HOLY VIRGINITY

O Wisdom, light of a pure mind, woe to them that leave your guidance and wander from your paths, who love your gestures instead of yourself, and are unmindful of what you suggest. For you do not cease to suggest what you are and how great, and your gestures are all the beauty of created things.

The workman, too, by the beauty of his work suggests to him who examines the work that he should not linger there, but should contemplate the visible shape of the material made so that he may turn back in appreciation to him who did the work.

They, then, who love the things that you do instead of yourself, are like men who hear some eloquent philosopher, but while eagerly paying attention to the charm of his voice, the structure of syllables and their proper stress, lose the commanding force of the sentences, of which the words were merely sounding signals.

Woe to them that turn away from your light, and cling contentedly only to their own shadow. For, turning their back on you, they are fixed in the shadow of their own work according to the flesh. And yet what really delights them there, they hold back from the full brightness of your light. When the shadow is loved, it makes the eye of the soul weak and less strong for the enjoyment of the sight of you.

FREE CHOICE OF THE WILL

LET us not speak in this earthly beauty what it has not received, for because it has not received what we seek it is on that account in the lowest place. But for what it has received let us praise God, since even to such a lowly thing he has given the great goodness of an outward beauty. Yet let us not cling to it as lovers of it, but let us pass beyond it as praisers of God, that, from somewhere above it, we may judge it, and not attached to it, be judged in it. And let us press onward to that good which is without any change of place, without any movement in time, and from which all natural things receive in place and time their form and appearance.

AGAINST THE FOUNDATION LETTER OF MANI

FIFTEEN

Soliloquies

THEE I invoke, O God, the Truth, in whom and from whom and through whom all things are true which anywhere are true. God, the Wisdom, in whom and from whom and through whom all things are wise which anywhere are wise. God, the true and crowning Life, in whom and from whom and through whom all things live, which truly and supremely live. God, the Blessedness, in whom and from whom and through whom all things are blessed, which anywhere are blessed. God, the Good and Fair, in whom and from whom and through whom all things are good and fair, which anywhere are good and fair. God, the intelligible Light, in whom and from whom and through whom all things intelligibly shine, which anywhere intelligibly shine. God, whose kingdom is that whole world of which sense has no ken. God, from whose kingdom a law is even derived down upon these lower realms. God, from whom to be turned away, is to fall: to whom to be turned back, is to rise again: in whom to abide, is to stand firm. God, from whom to go forth, is to die: to whom to return, is to revive: in whom to have our dwelling, is to live. God, whom no one loses, unless deceived: whom no one seeks, unless stirred up: whom no one finds, unless made pure. God, whom to forsake, is one thing with perishing; toward whom to tend, is one thing with living: whom to see is one thing with having. God, toward whom faith rouses us, hope lifts us up, with whom love joins us. God, through whom we overcome the enemy, thee I entreat. God, through whose gift it is, that we do not perish utterly. God, by whom we are warned to watch. God, by whom we distinguish good from ill. God, by whom we flee evil, and follow good. God, through whom we yield not to calamities. God, through whom we faithfully serve and benignantly govern. God, through whom we learn those things to be another's which aforetime we accounted ours, and those things to be ours which we used to account as belonging to another. God, through whom the baits and enticements of evil things have no power to hold us. God, through whom it is that diminished possessions leave ourselves complete. God, through whom our better good is not subject to a worse. God, through whom death is swallowed up in victory. God, who dost turn us to thyself. God, who dost strip us of that which is not, and arrayest us in that which is. God, who dost make us worthy to be heard. God, who dost fortify us. God, who leadest us into all truth. God, who speakest to us only good, who neither terrifiest into madness nor sufferest another so to do. God, who callest us back into the way. God, who leadest us to the door of life. God, who causest it to be opened to them that knock. God, who givest us the bread of life. God, through whom we thirst for the draft, which being drunk we never thirst. God, who dost convince the world of sin, of righteousness, and of judgment. God, through whom it is that we are not commoved by those who refuse to believe. God, through whom we disapprove the error of those, who think that there are no merits of souls before thee. God, through whom it comes that we are not in bondage to the weak and beggarly elements. God, who cleansest us, and preparest us for divine rewards, to me propitious come thou.

Whatever has been said by me, thou the only God, do thou come to my help, the one true and eternal substance, where is no discord, no confusion, no shifting, no indigence, no death. Where is supreme concord, supreme evidence, supreme steadfastness, supreme fullness, and life supreme. Where nothing is lacking, nothing redundant. Where Begetter and Begotten are one. God, whom all things serve, that serve, to whom is compliant every virtuous soul. By whose laws the poles revolve, the stars fulfill their courses, the sun vivifies the day, the moon tempers the night: and all the framework of things, day after day by vicissitude of light and gloom, month after month by waxings and wanings of the moon, year after year by orderly successions of spring and summer and fall and winter, cycle after cycle by accomplished concurrences of the solar course, and through the mighty orbs of time, folding and refolding upon themselves, as the stars still recur to their first conjunctions, maintains, so far as this merely visible matter allows, the mighty constancy of things. God, by whose ever-during laws the stable motion of shifting things is suffered to feel no perturbation, the thronging course of circling ages is ever recalled anew to the image of immovable quiet: by whose laws the choice of the soul is free, and to the good rewards and to the evil pains are distributed by necessities settled throughout the nature of everything. God, from whom distil even to us all benefits, by whom all evils are withheld from us. God, above whom is nothing, beyond whom is nothing, without whom is nothing. God, under whom is the whole, in whom is the whole, with whom is the whole. Who hast made man after thine image and likeness, which he discovers, who has come to know himself. Hear me, hear me, graciously hear me, my God, my Lord, my King, my Father, my Cause, my Hope, my Wealth, my Honor, my House, my Country, my Health, my Light, my Life. Hear, hear, hear me graciously, in that way, all thine own, which though known to few is to those few known so well.

Henceforth thee alone do I love, thee alone I follow, thee alone I seek, thee alone am I prepared to serve, for thou alone art Lord by a just title, of thy dominion do I desire to be. Direct, I pray, and command whatever thou wilt, but heal and open my ears, that I may hear thine utterances. Heal and open my eyes, that I may behold thy significations of command. Drive delusion from me, that I may recognize thee. Tell me whither I must tend, to behold thee, and I hope that I shall do all things thou mayest enjoin. O Lord, most merciful Father, receive, I pray, thy fugitive; enough already, surely, have I been punished, long enough have I served thine enemies, whom thou hast under thy feet, long enough have I been a sport of fallacies. Receive me fleeing from these, thy house-born servant, for did not these receive me, though another Master's, when I was fleeing from thee? To thee I feel I must return: I knock; may thy door be opened to me; teach me the way to thee. Nothing else have I than the will: nothing else do I know than that fleeting and falling things are to be spurned, fixed and everlasting things to be sought. This I do, Father, because this alone I know, but from what quarter to approach thee I do not know. Do thou instruct me, show me, give me my provision for the way. If it is by faith that those find thee, who take refuge with thee, then grant faith: if by virtue, virtue: if by knowledge, knowledge. Augment in me, faith, hope, and charity. O goodness of thine, singular and most to be admired!

SOLILOQUIES

GOD, always the same, let me know myself, let me know you. I have prayed. . . .

God our Father who exhort us to pray, who make it possible for us to pray, our entreaty is made to you, for when we pray to you we live better and we are better.

Hear me groping in these glooms, and stretch forth your right hand to me. Shed your light on me, call me back from my wanderings. Bring yourself into me so that I may in the same way return to you. Amen.

SOLILOQUIES

DEVOTIONAL AND TOPICAL INDEX

SOURCE AND NAME INDEX

F. FORRESTER CHURCH is Senior Minister of All Souls Unitarian Church in New York City. Editor of Macmillan's *The Essential Tillich* and author of *Father & Son, The Devil & Dr. Church, Entertaining Angels,* and *The Seven Deadly Virtues,* he also writes a weekly column for *The Chicago Tribune* on "Fundamentals" syndicated by Tribune Media Services. Dr. Church received his Ph.D. in 1978 from Harvard University in the field of Early Church History.

TERRENCE J. MULRY received his B.A. in Religion and master's degree in International Affairs from Columbia University, after which he worked for ten years in publishing. He is in his second year of the Master of Divinity program at Harvard Divinity School.